THE LAST CRUSADER

Vosper

John Cobb's World Water Speed Record Challenger.

By Barry Stobart-Hook.

To
Commander Peter Du Cane
and
Sir John Rix
without whose efforts there would have been no
Vosper Thornycroft, and no VT Group.

Published by April Cottage Publications.
ISBN 978-0-9559147-0-6
Copyright © B. Stobart-Hook 2008.
Printed by RPM Print & Design, Chichester UK.

Acknowledgements.

My grateful thanks to:

The VT Group for permission to use Vosper Company material from Cdr. Du Cane's files;

Castrol Film and Photographic Archives (formerly C.C.Wakefield Ltd), Mrs Francie Bradley on behalf of the Estate of Dr Willie 'Frank' Macdonald, Getty Images, Highland Photographic Archive - Highland Council, Motor Boat & Yachting, Qinetiq/A.E.W., Sir Anthony Quilter , Solent Sky, and Topfoto, for permission to use their images;

The Estate of the late Dr Ewen C.B. Corlett for access to his private memoir and the use of images;

Charles Du Cane for further images, information, advice, help and for writing the foreword;

Gordon Menzies, of Temple Pier, for the photo on page 128, access to his father's account of the events, and for handing on the story to succeeding generations;

And especially to Alan Macdonald, Bruce Shairp and Diana Royce of Architech in Inverness for designing the cover, proof reading and providing an enormous amount of information, advice and help, including their computer models on the front cover and page 72.

Every effort has been made to trace correct copyright holders, but due to the lapse of time and the existence of almost identical material from many different sources, there may have been omissions.

CONTENTS.

Foreword.

When Barry Stobart-Hook asked me to write a foreword for his book on the Crusader venture it brought back a whole plethora of memories of the life at Loch Ness during my school holidays in the summer of 1952. For me to be included in the party, living amongst the "good and the great", was to my young eyes a great privilege. John Cobb, an extremely quiet and gentle giant of a man, who answered the inevitable press questions with little more than a grunt, always had time and a kind word for the young. Not only where I was concerned, but also with the local school children. His young wife Vicki accompanied him. There was Reid Railton, an old friend of John Cobb, who had designed many of his famous record breaking cars, and Captain George Eyston who had been one his main competitors and through his position as a director of Castrol was recruited as the manager of the team involved with the record attempt at Loch Ness. Major Frank Halford from the de Havilland Company responsible for the design of the Ghost jet as well as many other engines was at Loch Ness with a team of engineers. There were many others who were equally important involved with the support of the venture whose names I simply do not remember. Enough for me to be in the company of these my childhood heroes!

Due to the team's reluctance to seek publicity and blow their trumpets before any records were achieved and the tragically sad circumstances that ended the venture, the story has remained somewhat distorted by wild speculation of underwater disturbances and even an encounter with the Loch Ness Monster! Barry Stobart-Hook, having had access to my father's private files, can now tell the whole story of the development and eventual running of Crusader. He has with infinite patience and thoroughness been able to sift the real story and record it with the accuracy it deserves.

The frustrations they had at Loch Ness with the weather, which was very similar to that we are experiencing in the summer of 2007, I am certain played its part in some of the decision making that occurred during the very long wait at Drumnadrochit. My father, having identified a weakness, wished to take the boat back to the Vosper shipyard at Portsmouth to strengthen the forward planing shoe, but the rest of the management team out voted him. As a result he then asked Cobb to keep the speed down to a maximum of 190mph and the rest of the story is told in detail in the book. Reid Railton also left a hand written comment in the margin of a book written about the record breakers: " Deformation of this surface had been noticed on the first runs, but we decided to risk it – fools that we were!"

As an after note I would like to add that this venture that had ended so sadly had brought my father in touch with Dick Wilkins, a senior stockjobber with Wedd Jefferson, who as a friend of John Cobb, was also an executor of his estate. Ten years later in 1962 Dick commissioned Vosper to build the first of a number of racing powerboats named Tramontana. That year she won the Daily Express International Trophy. Incidentally amongst the guests at a party given by Wilkins in Portsmouth for the Vosper team to celebrate the victory was George Eyston.

Charles Du Cane
July 2007

* * * * *

Prologue.

In September 1988 I was at a loose end. Having resigned my Executive Directorship of Vosper Thornycroft I was casting around for new things to do. One day, I happened to call at my old office about something or other. Carol, who had been my secretary but now worked for the Managing Director, wished me good morning. "Mr Usher has had a letter from Jean Carpenter," she said, "He wondered whether you could deal with it?".

In a bygone era, before the shipbuilding firms of Vosper and Thornycroft had merged, Jean had for many years occupied a similar position to that of Carol: She had been Personal Secretary to the great Commander Peter Du Cane, who had run Vosper Ltd since the 1930s, and had been largely responsible for creating the Company's reputation for designing and building fast boats, particularly small warships.

The great man's retirement had been a slow process, spread over several years during which he gradually relinquished his responsibilities, and spent more of his time on the various speed boat projects and associated activities which had become his hobby. Jean stayed on at Vosper, at first no doubt fully occupied with liasing between the Company and the Commander, but as his involvement gradually diminished and eventually ceased on his death, she spent more and more time on other matters. Organising all the foreign travel for the growing Company was becoming a full time job, and Jean, who had always done this anyway, became Travel Manager.

Now in retirement herself, she had several times contacted Peter Usher, saying that she had a number of old files in her attic which she thought should be returned to the Company. Her appeals had hitherto passed unanswered in the perpetual rush of a busy office. This time, however, her letter just happened to arrive in the office about the same time as I did.

In the preceding fifteen or twenty years, Jean had booked me on more flights to far away places than I could remember. As well as being a very efficient Travel Manager, she had always kept an eagle eye on the budget and woe betided anyone who showed the slightest prodigality whilst travelling on Company business. Regardless of their position in the Company, those who had overstepped the mark were left in no doubt as to Jean's views, and some quite senior managers had been known to tremble in their shoes when explaining their deeds to the Travel Manager! However, I had discovered long ago that her bark was infinitely worse than her bite, and welcomed an opportunity to see her again.

I found her house in a quiet Southsea street, and a little while later emerged staggering under half a dozen heavy box files, glad that I had been able to park my car nearby. Knowing full well that whatever they contained would at best end up unexamined in a dark corner of the Company library, or, worse still, perhaps be lost altogether, I agreed that I would retain the files for the time being, at least until I had been able to examine their contents, put them in some sort of order, and find a suitable long-term home for them.

A day or two later, I settled down to examine them. Choosing a box at random, I pulled out a dusty file. Papers and photographs spilled onto the floor and a name caught my eye. *Crusader*. It struck a distant and almost forgotten chord in my memory. Almost forty years earlier, I had stood, a twelve year old schoolboy, at the roadside, looking down at a clearing in the trees by a pier on the banks of Loch Ness. In the centre of the clearing a crowd of people were standing around a strange object on a trailer; a thirty foot long silver and red cigar, with floats jutting out like legs either side of its fat afterbody. In front and to each side of a small, open cockpit were two bulbous air intakes; like the eyes of some monstrous water beetle. Along the side of the trailer in bold letters was written: "John Cobb's *Crusader* designed and built by Vosper Ltd, Portsmouth."

In those days, every schoolboy had heard of John Cobb, the famous pre-war racing driver, who had twice broken the World Land Speed record and had travelled at 400 m.p.h. in a motor car. Now he was to attempt to break the Absolute Water Speed record, then held by an American at 178.4 m.p.h.

On several occasions over the following weeks my father and I rose very early in the morning and spent hours waiting by the loch. Two or three times we were rewarded with the eerie sound of the gas turbine echoing around the hills and the sight of *Crusader* hurtling along the loch, trailing a long plume of spray. It was after I had been packed off back to boarding school that a fellow pupil rushed into the library one afternoon. "Have you heard?" he cried "John Cobb's boat's blown up!"

Over the next few days we heard some details and saw the pictures in newspapers and magazines. There were weird and wonderful theories put forward which stirred the schoolboy imagination: In those days when aeroplanes had only recently flown faster than sound, "water barriers" and the like provided ample material for even the most unimaginative pressman. But nobody seemed to know what really had happened, and poor John Cobb and his unfulfilled ambition gradually faded from the headlines and from my memory. Now, so many years later, was the answer somewhere in these dusty files? Here were letters, press cuttings, reports, graphs, scribbled calculations on yellowing scraps of paper; the whole of Peter Du Cane's records from the very beginnings of the project until years after the end, when evidently there was still sporadic correspondence and the occasional magazine article which the Commander had carefully filed away.

That was not all. Also in the boxes, there was another treasure trove of paper relating to an older, pre-war speed king, Sir Malcolm Campbell, and his *Blue Bird*, the second boat of that name, of which I was only dimly aware. Like most people of my generation I had seen the news coverage of Sir Malcolm's son, Donald, over the years when he too had captured the Land Speed record and gone on to recapture the Water Speed record several times for Britain, in yet another *Blue Bird*. I remembered only too well the horrifically spectacular television coverage of *Blue Bird* somersaulting at around 300 m.p.h. before vanishing below the waters of Coniston, taking Donald Campbell with her. Both were to remain there until recovered in 2001.

It was clear that here was most of the material for one or more books, but at the time I was about to embark on writing a more recent history of Vosper Thornycroft, and even when that was eventually finished other projects took most of my attention, so Peter Du Cane's files became a very long term project.

I began to try to piece the story together but even when I had sorted them into chronological order (there were originally separate files for each correspondent or company), it was difficult to follow the many different threads without constant reference backwards and forwards through the papers and eventually I decided that the best approach would be to transcribe virtually everything onto a computer, making it more legible, accessible and editable whilst at the same time enabling me to get thoroughly familiar with the whole story. The main problem with this was that there was a huge volume of material, almost none of which was susceptible to text recognition programs, being mostly carbon copies, handwriting, or otherwise indistinct printing.

This process has therefore taken several years, as I was not prepared to spend all my available time on it! After finishing the *Blue Bird* files I put together an edited version of them, interspersed where necessary with additional text to bridge gaps or précis long documents. The result was at least reasonably coherent but perhaps of rather limited appeal, and was only circulated privately to a very limited number of readers, most of whom are ex-Vosper employees, or who were involved in the project in some way.

The *Crusader* files were much more bulky but nevertheless I decided to treat them similarly. I had completed perhaps half the task when I was contacted by Alan Macdonald and Diana Royce of Architech, who specialised in producing films using a mixture of computer modelling and real life to illustrate architectural projects. Based in Inverness, they had heard a lot about John Cobb and his boat, and decided to apply their rather unusual skills to making a film about *Crusader*. Enquiries soon led them to me, and fortunately I was able to supply them with a great deal of information, including drawings and photographs. I was also able to help them obtain further information through my remaining contacts with Vosper Thornycroft, who were most helpful.

Architech's energy and enthusiasm prompted me to speed up the process of transcribing the files, and inevitably I had again to consider what, if anything, to do with the results. The entire collection of transcribed files was much bulkier than the *Blue Bird* ones, and even an edited version was probably going to be not only lengthy but, at best, of very limited interest except to the same small number of individuals.

It therefore seemed that the only sensible course was to revert to the original plan of writing a book, a task for which I was at least now better equipped having not only become very familiar with the contents of the files, but also having the benefit of Diana's extensive research. Last but by no means least, through her I have met four other small boys who were at Loch Ness in the late summer of 1952: Charles Du Cane, son of the designer, who was small enough then to crawl inside *Crusader* and help with repairs; Dennis Cronk, son of Vosper's Chief Engineer, who was similarly qualified and not only helped likewise but also somehow avoided being sent back to school and so witnessed the final run; Richard Noble, who was inspired by the sight of *Crusader* to go out years later and break the Land Speed Record himself, and Gordon Menzies, current owner of Temple Pier who in 1952 helped his father Alec by fiercely guarding the entrance against uninvited Pressmen! Thanks are due to all of these, amongst several others, for information and encouragement.

These then, are the author's credentials. Now to get on with the story.

Barry Stobart-Hook

Half a century later, at the John Cobb Memorial, Loch Ness:
Richard Noble, Gordon Menzies, Dennis Cronk, Charles Du Cane.

Origins of the Water Speed Record.

Before beginning the story of John Cobb's jet boat, it would be appropriate to review its origins. The *Crusader* project might be said to have roots at around the beginning of the 20th century, when the internal combustion engine became a practical proposition and the business of record breaking began. In 1900 the land speed record stood at 65 m.p.h., modest enough by today's standards but an incredible speed for a world which, despite railways, still relied heavily on horses. By 1914 this figure had almost doubled, and although the Great War put a stop to record breaking for a few years, it lent impetus to technical development and provided a great source of surplus machinery with which young men could amuse themselves when peace came.

Blue Bird car 1934   *Hulton/Getty Images*

In the 20 years between the wars the land speed record went from 124 m.p.h. to 369 m.p.h., the average "life" of each new record being less than a year. The water speed record was less popular, and in the same period went from 61 to 141 m.p.h. in some 15 steps. Several of the land speed record contenders "retired" from their cars and took to boating in attempts to achieve the double, but although the speeds were lower, it soon became clear that water was not an easy option. Sir Henry Segrave, first to take the land speed record to over 200m.p.h., and later to over 230, was killed in 1930 at just over 100 m.p.h. when *Miss England II* capsized on Windemere, probably due to structural weakness of the forward step, although at the time it was assumed that he struck a floating log. *Miss England II* was repaired and with her Kay Don, a well known Brooklands racing driver, took the record to 120 m.p.h. in three steps, competing with the American Gar Wood who eventually held it from 1932 until 1937.

By 1935 Sir Malcolm Campbell had raised the land speed record to 301 m.p.h., having broken it no less than 12 times, (although some of his earlier records were unofficial due to timing technicalities) in various cars, which he invariably christened *"Blue Bird"*, written as two words and with no number following, although the press and nearly everyone else insisted otherwise. At this point he too decided to turn to the water, and had the first *"Blue Bird"* boat designed by Fred Cooper, who had been responsible for *"Miss England II"*.

The first *Blue Bird* boat   *Hulton/Getty Images*

This *Blue Bird* was built by Saunders-Roe, and was a single stepped hydroplane powered by a Rolls-Royce R type engine removed from one of the *Blue Bird* cars. After an unsuccessful but promising run on Loch Lomond, which proved to be rather rough, in 1937 Campbell took the boat to Locarno in Italy. Cooling problems caused engine failure, but a spare engine, also from one of the cars, was fitted and the record was increased to 129 m.p.h. However, at this speed *Blue Bird* was beginning to show signs of instability and Campbell was already considering another boat.

Reid Railton was the Chief Engineer of Thompson & Taylor Ltd, of Brooklands racing fame, and had designed most of Campbell's successful cars. As a close friend and technical adviser, he drew Sir Malcolm's attention to a small American speedboat designed by a man called Apel and built in the Ventnor boat works. This rode on two forward planing surfaces and the transom aft, and thus was a "three pointer", possessing inherent stability, rather like a three legged stool. Campbell bought one of these boats and had it shipped back to England, where he commissioned Cooper to design a record breaker based on this principle.

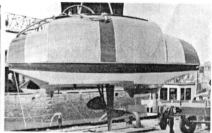

Ventnor hydroplane

Perhaps because Campbell was sometimes a difficult man to deal with, or perhaps because he was dissatisfied with the behaviour of his first *Blue Bird* boat, Cooper did not proceed very far with the new design before the two of them apparently fell out, and Campbell was left with a basic drawing, a model and a draft specification, and he and Railton were faced with the task of finding another boat designer.

Vosper Ltd. had been marine engineers in Camber docks, at the entrance to Portsmouth Harbour, since the 1870s, and later built various small craft, but it was not until 1930, when the same Fred Cooper who had designed *"Miss England II"*, joined the company, that Vosper began to take an interest in fast craft.

In 1931 Commander Peter Du Cane, an ex Naval Engineer, joined Vosper, and shortly afterwards became managing director. When Cooper left in 1933, Du Cane took over personal responsibility for design, and his expertise in fast craft was largely responsible for the success of the company in later years. By 1938 Vosper already had a reputation for designing and building small, fast craft including racing boats and naval and air force tenders, and was getting involved in Motor Torpedo Boat design and construction.

It was not therefore surprising that in June 1938 Du Cane received a letter from Sir Malcolm Campbell saying that there was a matter which he would very much like to discuss and which he thought would be of considerable interest.

Commander Peter Du Cane

Campbell came straight to the point and a few days later Du Cane found himself driving the little Ventnor hydroplane, which had been stored at a boatyard in nearby Southampton. He managed to do 64 m.p.h. without using full throttle and believed that she would probably do over 70 when pushed. He also considered that stability was better than that of the boats designed by Cooper.

He was impressed with the boat, and keen for Vosper Ltd to get the job of building a larger and better one. Not only would it be a very interesting project, but a potentially prestigious one for what was then a relatively small company still trying to make its mark in the fast boat field. Before the end of June he had agreed with Sir Malcolm that Vosper would work under the general technical supervision of Railton in conjunction with the Admiralty Experiment Works (A.E.W.) at nearby Haslar, Gosport. The task was to continue the work begun by Cooper to develop a record breaking hull based on the three point principle. The recently appointed Superintendent of A.E.W. was Dr. R.W.L.Gawn, a very distinguished member of the Royal Corps of Naval Constructors with a great deal of experience both on the staff of the Director of Naval Construction and at sea. He was to provide Du Cane with much vital help and support with Campbells' projects and, later, with John Cobb's *Crusader*. A.E.W. possessed facilities for towing ship models in a large tank, which Cooper and Du Cane were able to make use of when pressure of Admiralty work permitted. Railton met Du Cane there on the next available Saturday afternoon.

Dr Gawn   *A.E.W./Qinetic*

It might be as well at this point to explain briefly the principles of ship model testing. This technique, essential to modern ship design, was developed in the 1860s by William Froude, using a testing tank in Torquay which the Admiralty funded for him. In 1886 his son, Robert Edmund Froude transferred this Admiralty Experimental Workshop to the new facility at Haslar.

The shape, displacement and centre of gravity of a boat all have a considerable effect upon the resistance which the water offers to it when under way. Since these properties are difficult or impossible to change after construction, it is important to know in advance how a new design will perform, and, amongst other things, whether the available engines will drive it at the required speed.

A good deal of the necessary information can be obtained by building a reduced size model of the same shape, which will float at the same waterline as the projected design. If this model is then moved through the water, it will behave in a similar manner to the full size ship, and such things as wave patterns and the drag of the full size can be deduced.

The mathematical relationship between the model and the full size ship is known as Froude's Law, and states that for them to behave in a comparable manner, their speeds must be in the ratio not of their lengths (as might perhaps be expected), but of the square root of their lengths. Thus a one twenty-fifth scale model of a two hundred and fifty foot long ship designed to travel at twenty knots, will be ten feet long, and must move at four knots to simulate the real thing.

This example is a relatively practical proposition, but in the case of a twenty seven foot long hydroplane designed to travel at 150 m.p.h., an 1/8th scale model (just over 3 ft long) would have to be towed at 53 m.p.h., or nearly 80 feet per second.

A test tank has to be several hundred feet long to allow a reasonable length of run. Models are usually towed by a carriage which straddles the tank and carries men, cameras and other equipment to observe and record the run. This weighty collection requires quite a lot of power and a good deal of space in which to accelerate to the required speed and eventually to stop again before reaching the far end. It is not difficult to see why towing tanks are very large and expensive facilities, and why Haslar's maximum speed of around 40 feet per second (27 m.p.h.) was (and still is) a very respectable figure.

For 40 feet per second to represent a full scale speed of 150 m.p.h. would require a 1/30 scale model, which would only have been about ten inches long. This is too small to be a practical proposition; for example, some of the forces acting on it would be too small to measure accurately. There is thus a limit to the full size speeds which can be represented in this way.

AEW Haslar; No.1 Ship Tank   *A.E.W./Qinetic*

Cooper's available 1/8th scale model could represent a full scale speed of about 70 m.p.h. It was described by du Cane as "rectangular"; probably consisting solely of three rectangular planing surfaces connected together, representing only those parts of the boat in contact with the water. In any event, at that first Saturday session at Haslar, tests proved unsatisfactory, and it was decided to construct another model, this time to 1/16th scale, which could simulate a speed of around 100 m.p.h. As they were aiming at speeds in excess of 150 m.p.h., this was still a compromise which would require results to be extrapolated.

Thus began what was to be a lengthy design process involving several models. Although Cooper's original model proved unsatisfactory, it was not long before they achieved promising towing tank results and Railton, who was also heavily engaged in John Cobb's first land speed record attempt in the

Railton Mobil Special at Bonneville, Utah, departed for America thinking that full size boat design could commence. He had agreed that whilst there he would consult Apel on the topic of three pointers.

Du Cane however was still not entirely satisfied with the hull design and embarked on further modifications. He was also concerned about potential aerodynamic problems. The wide forebody of the new three-point design, resulting from the two forward planing surfaces, or sponsons, allowed air to flow under and over the central hull with the obvious possibility of generating lift, which ultimately might flip the boat onto its back. Exchanging telegrams with Railton, he learned that Apel was well aware of this, but thought that a limited amount of lift was beneficial, because it reduced the effective displacement.

Model tests, particularly on a small model, do not accurately reproduce full size aerodynamics at the speed required by hydrodynamic considerations. Separate trials in a wind tunnel at the Vickers aircraft works were therefore necessary, and these showed a clear danger of the boat trying to "fly" at the speeds contemplated. Henceforth these effects had to be taken into consideration, and were to have a dominant influence on the design of *Crusader*. Thirty years later they were what killed Sir Malcolm's son, Donald, when another *Blue Bird* "flew" at nearly 300 m.p.h.

Back in 1938 they were only aiming at about 160m.p.h., and eventually Vickers aerodynamicists arrived at a satisfactory shape for the topsides. All this time Campbell was urging Du Cane to start building the boat, but the latter refused to be rushed until he was entirely satisfied with the model results.

It was intended to use the engine, gearbox and propeller shaft from the existing *Blue Bird*, partly to save money, but also on the sound principle of changing only one thing at a time (the hull) in order to assess the effect clearly. Campbell meanwhile was keen to make a further attempt in the old boat and took it to Lac Leman, at Geneva, and then to Hallwil, near Lucerne, where he eventually succeeded in raising his previous record by 1.4 m.p.h. to 130.9, with some help from Du Cane, who had an opportunity to drive the boat and see for himself the problems which prevented this hull from being driven any faster. Campbell, who was not really technical, ascribed his problems to underwater springs, the wake of steamers on the lake, and the fact that *Blue Bird* had only a single screw, causing torque reaction problems which he suggested should be cured by fitting two shafts to the new boat. He also passed on to Du Cane several letters from well-meaning but misguided cranks, who by now had heard of his plans to build a new boat and were keen to offer suggestions. These made diverting reading, but were in no way helpful.

Du Cane knew that most of the problems could be cured by the new hull and correct propeller design, and wisely stuck to his principle of changing as little as possible at once.

Despite all of this, and his habit of arguing furiously over every bill, Campbell continued to be impatient at every delay, the more so because he could see the strong possibility of war with Nazi Germany putting a stop to all such endeavours.

1/25th Scale *Blue Bird* model   *A.E.W./Qinetic*

16

At last Du Cane was satisfied with the design, and as a final check a 1/25th scale model was constructed and towed in the tank at an equivalent speed of 145 m.p.h. This model is still held at Haslar today. Although too small to permit accurate drag measurements, it at least boosted confidence by behaving in a satisfactorily stable manner, and so construction of the full size boat began towards the end of October 1938, at about the same time as Railton returned from America.

The engine, gearbox and shafting were removed from the old boat and re-installed in the new one by Thompson & Taylor at Brooklands, and in August 1939 the completed boat finally arrived at Coniston. After only a few preparatory runs *Blue Bird* broke the record by a handsome 11 m.p.h., setting it at 141. A week later, war was declared.

Although obviously heavily preoccupied with other matters, Campbell and Du Cane remained in touch throughout the war, and as it gradually became clear who was going to win, Campbell became more and more impatient to resume the important business of record breaking. But even when peace resumed and there were thousands of surplus aero engines in existence, they all seemed still to be on the secret list and Rolls-Royce were far too interested in recovering from the war and chasing export markets to divert vital expertise to help Sir Malcolm Campbell.

The record run: *Blue Bird* 1939   *Vosper*

It seemed likely that a little more performance could still be squeezed out of Sir Malcolm's now obsolete Rolls-Royce R type engines, (which dated back to 1930) but just how much remained a mystery because nobody knew exactly what power had been developed by the record breaking engine, nor how much more might be available from the other ones in Sir Malcolm's possession. Relevant Rolls Royce records had been destroyed, and although Du Cane believed that some improvement was likely, it hardly seemed worth the effort and expense.

At last, however, an old friend of Sir Malcolm came to the rescue. Frank Halford of the De Havilland engine company, who were successfully involved in aeronautical record breaking, arranged for the loan of a Goblin jet engine, belonging to the Ministry of Supply. This was an exciting offer, but presented several problems: Nobody had tried a jet engine in a boat before, and to accommodate the Goblin and the resulting different thrust line meant a radical redesign of the boat. Then came the aerodynamics; the necessary structural changes and the anticipated increase in speed meant a complete redesign of the superstructure. Questions were also raised concerning the recognition of any record which might be claimed by a boat which was not propelled by a water screw.

Du Cane tackled all these problems in his usual methodical way. This time, as Vickers were very busy, aerodynamic advice and wind tunnel testing were provided by Fairey Aviation, with Campbell impatiently waiting, worried that "his" record was under threat by the Americans. At last the boat was ready and Du Cane tried to persuade Campbell to carry out preliminary trials in Poole Harbour, away from the Press and as near as possible to Vospers Yard. However, following a Press day at the Yard when the boat was unveiled, Campbell decided to go straight to Coniston with the completely untried boat.

The result was a fiasco which received the full attention of the Press. The boat turned out to be unstable in both yaw and pitch – it skidded and porpoised – and had to return to Vospers. Du Cane made some modifications, this time persuading Campbell to test the boat at Poole, where as soon as it was clear that the skidding had been cured Campbell rushed back to Coniston where the Press again assembled. Du Cane, who was abroad on other business, almost immediately received a frantic message asking him to return as the boat was still porpoising at the higher speeds obtainable on Coniston.

Relaunch of *Blue Bird* with a jet engine, 1947   *Vosper*

Porpoising is a complicated form of instability which can occur in fast boats or seaplanes, and is a combination of pitching (movement about a transverse horizontal axis with the bow and stern alternately rising and falling) and heaving (when the whole boat moves vertically up and down.) It is self-sustaining and can become quite violent. It is obviously undesirable, and, in 1947 at least, was not well understood.

By July 1947, De Havilland were being pressed by the Ministry of Supply for return of their engine, but Halford managed to obtain an extension of the loan, although he was not pleased at the public failures and stipulated that that there should be further discreet trials at Poole before a further public record attempt. Campbell did not favour this, partly because of his natural impatience and partly because he considered that he had been overcharged for the use of facilities at Poole.

Du Cane, with the assistance of Dr. Gawn at A.E.W. Haslar, continued to seek the solution of the porpoising problem, which proved impossible to reproduce in the models. Various theories were advanced to explain this, including the effects of air being sucked into the forward intakes, and the inability of the model towing arrangements accurately to reproduce the effect of the jet thrust. At this point, Railton, who had been sent to America during the war on assignment for the Admiralty, and had later emigrated permanently, re-established contact by letter and offered a few suggestions, although he himself commented that this was very difficult from the far side of the Atlantic.

Some modifications were eventually made to the boat and preparations made for more trials at Poole, but at this point Campbell received a letter from Canada, inviting him to bring his new boat for trials in Vancouver. Despite protests from Du Cane and Halford, who could not see any sense in taking the boat 6000 miles away to see if it still porpoised, he announced that he had decided to accept this invitation, despite the fact that the problems were still unsolved. Moreover, anticipating Halfords opposition to this idea, he had approached the Ministry of Supply direct to try to obtain a Goblin engine independently. When Halford inevitably heard of this, it was the last straw, and in June 1948 De Havilland withdrew their support and the engine, thus effectively putting an end to the project.

Sadly, Campbell, whose health had been failing, died soon afterwards on 31st December 1948. His son Donald, took over *Blue Bird,* re-installed the old Rolls Royce engine, and later modified her as a "prop rider", using a surface piercing propeller. Meanwhile the Americans had raised the record to 160 m.p.h. with a prop rider called *Slo-Mo-Shun IV*. In September 1951, after more modifications, Donald reached an unofficially estimated 170m.p.h., when a blade came off the propeller, possibly due to hitting a floating obstruction: The unbalanced drive shaft tore through the hull and sank the boat, which was finally written off.

Donald's subsequent career with a new jet propelled *Blue Bird* designed by the Norris brothers is well documented. Both Du Cane and Railton had provided some help and advice in modifying the old *Blue Bird,* but by then both were becoming involved with John Cobb's project, and had little or nothing to do with Donalds' successful record breaking.

An egg with legs.

It is now necessary to go back in time a little, to mid 1947, when Du Cane was becoming increasingly enthusiastic about jet propulsion for the Worlds Water Speed Record. He had also reached several other conclusions:

First, he had misgivings about the three point layout of *Blue Bird* on account of the inherent aerodynamic lift. With two of the three "points" at the front, the centre of lift was well placed to raise the bow, which tended to increase the lift further and begin a vicious circle leading to a backward somersault. Robert, Du Canes' younger brother, remembers suggesting a reversed arrangement so that there were two points at the stern and only one forward, thus moving the centre of aerodynamic lift aft and reducing the bows up pitching moment. Railton too was independently to think of this.

Secondly, it would in any case be preferable to design a new boat from scratch for this purpose, rather than to modify one designed almost ten years before for screw propulsion and a lower speed range.

Finally, Du Cane concluded that the increasingly infirm Sir Malcolm was not the best man to drive such a boat.

He confided these views to Frank Halford, saying that he hoped one day that the two of them could get together on such a project. In the meantime however, he continued to do his best for Campbell for over a year, despite the fact that the latter was beginning to try everybody's patience severely.

In late 1947 Du Cane wrote to Dr. Gawn of A.E.W., asking for a rough estimate of how fast a hard chine hull of about 7000lb. displacement might travel if propelled by a jet engine of 5000lb thrust. Gawn replied that this was an academic question as it would be substantially airborne at around 180 m.p.h., and beyond that would overturn. However, he estimated that resistance would be aerodynamic drag plus that of any fins or rudders, and guessed that about 210 m.p.h. might be achieved. This reply was about what was expected by Du Cane, who considered that it ought to be possible to design an aerodynamically neutral body, which would not fly.

By mid 1948, shortly after De Havilland had finally fallen out with Campbell, he had roughed out some lines and a model, which he showed to Halford and to Mike Hooper, of Fairey Aviation, who had done most of the wind tunnel tests on the jet *Blue Bird.* Although no drawings of this model seem to have survived, it appears to have been a stepless hard chine form. Halford was interested, but made the obvious comment that it was not the right time to approach his Board for the loan of another jet engine!

To Hooper, Du Cane commented that although this model was not particularly efficient hydrodynamically, he believed that if it the aerodynamics were reasonable, they would be on the right track. Hooper made a few suggestions on modifying the superstructure.

At about this time – late summer 1948 – there were two important developments; John Cobb and "Jetex" motors appeared on the scene.

John Cobb.

In August 1939, the former had taken the Land Speed Record to 369 m.p.h. in a car designed by Reid Railton, and in

September 1947 had returned, with Railton, to Utah and raised it further to 394 m.p.h., exceeding 400m.p.h. in one direction, becoming the first man so to do. Cobb was at this time the undisputed land speed king, and his record was to stand for the next seventeen years. Probably while in Utah awaiting suitable running conditions he and Railton had turned their thoughts to attempting the double, the water speed record being an obvious challenge for his love of speed and technical innovation. The recent tragic loss of his wife of only fourteen months to Brights disease had only increased his need to immerse himself in something new. Now he was definitely interested in a jet propelled boat, and approached Du Cane, mentioning that he had also had an interesting chat with Halford. This seemed to imply that although currently unable to promise anything, the latter remained sympathetic and open to future approaches.

Jetex motors offered a useful means of testing boat models at the required speeds. They were small rocket motors produced by Wilmot & Mansour of Totton, near Southampton, and were intended to power model aeroplanes. Du Cane had built such a model for his children, and was impressed when it flew away in the direction of Chichester, and was never seen again. During the attempts to reproduce the behaviour of the jet propelled *Blue Bird* at model scale, Railton had suggested using a small cylinder of carbon dioxide as a rocket motor, and Jetex offered an admirable refinement of this idea. Although it was difficult or impossible to measure the speed or resistance of a free running rocket driven model, general behaviour and stability could be checked at speeds far in excess of what could be achieved with the towing carriage.

The production Jetex motors were too small to drive models of the size Du Cane wanted, so Wilmot and Mansour offered to produce a larger version to special order, with a thrust of about 1lb. Whilst they were doing this, they lent Du Cane a slightly less powerful prototype to enable him and A.E.W. to develop this new model testing technique.

They began by testing models of *Blue Bird* and his new hard chine design. One objective was of course to investigate the elusive porpoising phenomenon. Interestingly, the hard chine model porpoised severely, and the *Blue Bird* model, whilst still refusing to porpoise, demonstrated the aerodynamic effect by turning over at an equivalent speed of 170 m.p.h.!

In April 1949 Du Cane wrote to Railton in America, describing all this and saying that the porpoising was still a very perplexing problem. He reported that John Cobb was very keen on the jet proposition, and that he, Du Cane, had agreed to work for Cobb, with Railton, on the project. He also asked Railton for recent intelligence on fast boat development in America, in particular about a boat called *Miss Canada* which had appeared in the yachting press.

Reid Railton

Hulton/Getty Images

Cobb now asked Du Cane not to work with anyone else on a similar job, which was agreed: De Havilland had in any case just turned down a request from Donald Campbell for a further loan of the Goblin jet engine. Cobb had heard a rumour that *Blue Bird* was for sale, and expressed mild interest, but the rumour was unfounded as Donald was determined by then to put the old R type engine back and have another go.

Railton wrote back to Du Cane enthusiastically saying that he hoped that Du Cane, Cobb and he could get together and work something out. He too had been approached by Donald and whilst not wishing to be unhelpful was slightly embarrassed because of his association with Cobb. However, he was convinced that although it had been reasonable to persevere with *Blue Bird* whilst Sir Malcolm was alive, he now thought that more work on that hull would be a waste of time and energy.

It seemed to him now, he wrote to Du Cane, that the aerodynamic problem was the whole crux of the matter. Suggesting a minimum target of 200 m.p.h., his approach would be to start by designing a body which would be safe aerodynamically at 250 m.p.h. as well as having sufficient space for the pilot and engine, and only then to work in the necessary buoyancy and planing surfaces. He envisaged something like a seaplane hull but with two small floats or skis mounted on outriggers at the stern. In other words, he continued, "a tricycle with the one wheel in front"

This was typical of Railton's innovative engineering approach, and Du Cane later cited this letter as the original conceptual design for *Crusader*. However, without in any way detracting from Railton's contribution, it is clear from previous records that Du Cane was already working on very similar lines. Railton was convinced that the approach which he outlined was correct; his worries being that Vosper might not wish to be associated with something which might end up more like an aeroplane than a boat, and for similar reasons, support from A.E.W. might not be forthcoming. He was also well aware of the need for suitable propulsion, but felt that in due course "we could soon pry an engine loose somewhere."

In the event, he need not have worried on either count: Du Cane wrote back to agree with this approach and assure him that both Vosper and the Director of Naval Construction would give it their support. Cobb also kept up the pressure on De Havilland, and although Halford wrote to Du Cane repeating that the time was still not ripe to raise the matter again, he continued to express interest and thought that in due course something could be done.

Railton was not the only one to offer suggestions. In early June 1949 Du Cane received a letter signed "Rod Banks", enclosing a sketch of an imaginary jet propelled catamaran. He had dealt with Air Commodore Rodwell Banks, the Ministry's Director of Aero engine production, towards the end of the war when seeking suitable piston engines for Sir Malcolm Campbell's post war ambitions. Banks was an expert in aviation fuels who had contributed significantly to the success of the British Schneider Trophy seaplanes in the early 1930s. Although his letter was written in a light hearted manner, describing the sketch as his "nightmare", it was far from being frivolous. It showed a catamaran formed of two floats joined by an arch carrying the pilot and jet engine, Banks explaining that the object was to produce a boat of extreme stability with good aerodynamic characteristics. It was, he wrote, probably crazy and would end up in Du Cane's waste-paper basket. There is no record of Du Cane's reply, but at least it did not suffer this fate! In 1949 a jet propelled catamaran was years ahead of its time. The little sketch looks remarkably like some modern race boats.

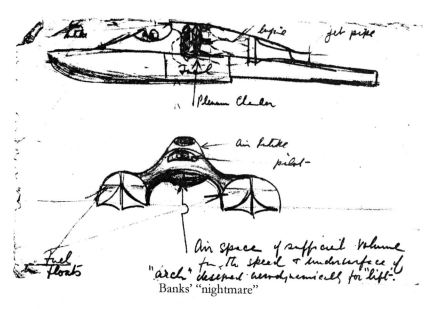

Banks' "nightmare"

In his continuing endeavours to solve the porpoising mystery, Du Cane approached Mr. Perring, Director of the Royal Aircraft Establishment at Farnborough, whom he later described as the greatest living expert on the subject. He reported their discussion to Cobb as "highly illuminating but not altogether encouraging."

Nevertheless, he now embarked on the long series of model trials which would eventually lead to a practical design for John Cobb. He wrote:

    I first schemed a lay-out incorporating an obviously good though somewhat impractical aerodynamic form of sufficient size to house pilot, engine and fuel. The aim here was to produce an aerodynamic form so that when the craft was running steadily at the designed trim there would be no tendency either to lift or depress.

    Furthermore in the event that a disturbance such as a wave or "swell" causes the whole craft to assume an angle likely to cause lift it is then desirable to select a shape so that the resultant of forces due to lift and drag act in such a direction as to restore the running trim angle rather than increase it.

    On to this nacelle or hull were attached four legs with aluminium skis attached to the lower extremities, in such a manner that their angle of incidence could be varied, as well as the spread and span. The fourth leg was located aft with the object of damping out any inherent tendency to "porpoise."

    After some fairly considerable running of this model (in the towing tank at first) a combination of angles and other dimensions emerged which appeared likely to give stable running conditions at speed. This latter consideration was thought to be of more importance at this stage than was the achievement of maximum propulsive efficiency. In the course of this process the fourth leg was found to be redundant.

The "Egg on legs"

    In the case of the three-legged model an air rudder or fin was selected to assist in keeping the free model straight. This was because only small water fins could be incorporated on to the skis.

    The results were promising in that steady and stable running combined with good planing area reducing qualities was achieved. In the course of tests the optimum angles of incidence for forward and aft skis were obtained, following these initial trials this model was fitted with a model rocket unit capable of exerting the scale thrust appropriate to the dimensional scale of the model.

In order to launch the model it became necessary to run it down a launching ramp as it was not thought at first that this type of model would be capable of lifting itself from static floating position on to the skis.

While considerable trouble was experienced in obtaining reliable running of this model, there were on a few occasions such startlingly good results that it was felt desirable to pursue this line of development.

A.E.W. were now using the rocket motors in their tank at Haslar, but many of the trials with the self propelled models took place in Vosper's wet dock at their Portchester Shipyard, or on the nearby upper reaches of Portsmouth Harbour when calm enough.

Although this "Egg on legs" model was only ever intended as the first stage and was clearly unsuitable without further development, valuable lessons were learnt. The porpoising effect was still not fully understood either by A.E.W. or Vospers, or apparently for that matter by anyone else, but Du Cane had learned that there was an unexplained but effective convention in flying boat design that buttock lines should be kept straight for about 10 per cent of the hull length ahead of the step. Whilst he was not entirely convinced by this, his skis effectively incorporated this property. He also arranged for the forward planing surface to be relatively heavily loaded, also in order to discourage porpoising.

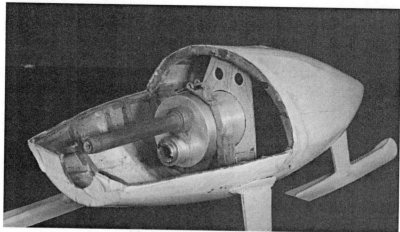

The Jetex motor installation

In spite of the problems experienced in obtaining reliable running of the "Egg", it was well that they persevered because it later became clear that this configuration of surfaces was the correct one and, although it was not realised at the time, the inconsistent results were largely due to a totally different cause.

This was the stage which had been reached in late August 1949 when Railton arrived from America and became actively involved in the next stage of model tests. This would necessitate more models and further use of the Haslar tank, and as the emphasis had now definitely shifted from *Blue Bird* and porpoising studies to the new design, Du Cane wrote to Sir Charles Lillicrap, the Director of Naval Construction, outlining John Cobb's intentions and seeking D.N.C.'s continued approval for support by Gawn and his establishment. Sir Charles wrote back that he would be very glad to do all that he could to help in this new project.

Du Cane demonstrated the "Egg" to Railton and Cobb, who agreed that the aerodynamics and general running were promising, but that obviously something had to be done to solve the starting problem, as the pilot could hardly be expected to launch the boat and himself down a ramp. Also of course he would next be faced with the question of what to do when the boat slowed down!

The starting problem of course consisted of getting over what is referred to as the "hump". This is a problem faced by all fast planing hulls. Obviously, when at rest, the boat has to displace water and float. When it first begins to move it must continue to displace water, which must be pushed out of the way. As speed increases, so does the force required to do this; the drag rises rapidly. But as speed increases the planing surfaces begin to generate significant lift, and the hull starts to rise out of the water, thus reducing the displacement and therefore the drag. Eventually the hull is almost completely clear of the surface and is supported entirely by the force of water striking the planing surfaces. Thus it may be seen that as the boat speed increases, the drag at first increases and then begins to decrease: This is the "hump", which requires effort to overcome.

In the case of the "egg", it was buoyant when at rest, and optimised both aero- and hydro-dynamically at high speed, but quite incapable of getting over the hump unaided. Solving this problem would inevitably involve some compromise.

The first move towards the development of a more practical form was to shorten the length of the legs and thus the water clearance, resulting in what Du Cane referred to in another paper as version "A": (the accompanying sketches are from Du Canes own original freehand drawings)

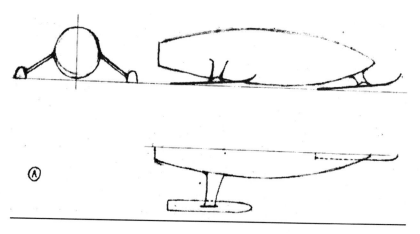

Although this did not solve the problem, it proved workable and was a step in the right direction. Railton suggested the next model, "B", which added buoyancy to the planing surfaces, and made them smaller, presumably to minimise adverse effects on the aerodynamics. A 1/6th model was made for the express purpose of checking this in the wind tunnel.

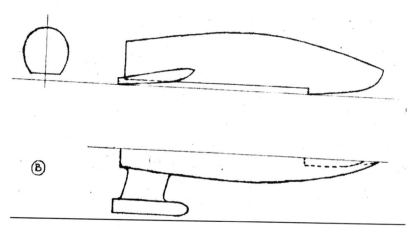

Fairey Aviation, who had tested the aerodynamics of the jet propelled *Blue Bird*, had kindly agreed to carry out at least some preliminary wind tunnel tests free of charge, and so at the same time Railton suggested taking a further step by integrating the aft sponsons with the hull, as in model "C", which was also sent for testing in the wind tunnel. Unfortunately he had to return to America in October 1949 before all these trials were completed.

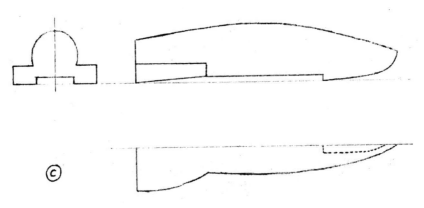

The results of these tests made it clear that for aerodynamic reasons the sponsons should be separated from the main hull. Nevertheless version "C" was tried as a free running 1/16th model with Jetex propulsion, but proved to be transversely unstable anyway, apparently because the aft planing surfaces were too close together.

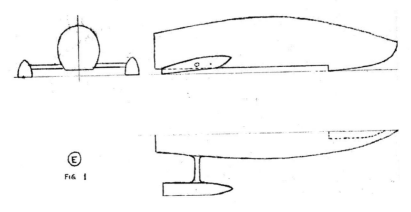

In an attempt to improve this model, the sponsons were separated from the hull and moved further apart, resulting in "E"

(There does not seem to have been a "D"). Thus began a series of trials, resulting in several different models, some of which went through a number of modification states.

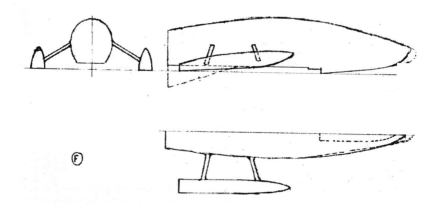

There are many photographs of models, some graphs of their performance, and frequent references to them in correspondence and reports. Unfortunately, despite efforts by Haslar to rationalise the nomenclature, Vosper used a different and less disciplined system, so that it is now far from clear which model was which, and thus some details of their development are impossible to reconstruct accurately. Some points are however clear:

Du Cane had difficulty with version "E" and therefore tried "F", which used exactly the same planing surfaces as the "Egg". This necessitated building a different model with longer sponsons and a longer surface faired into the bow.

This series of models were to be designated CJK by Haslar, and by June 1950 eleven different variants had been produced, the final one being CJK11. These were, probably, all derivatives of models "E" or "F", each of which was progressively modified.

For directional stability the large aerodynamic fin of the "Egg" was replaced by water fins, in most cases on the inner edge of each of the aft planing surfaces. In a full sized boat with a human pilot these could be further reduced in size as control would be by means of a single rudder attached to the back of the forward surface. A moment's thought indicates that, because this would be forward of the centre of lateral resistance, it would have to be deflected in the opposite direction to the desired turn; unconventional but perfectly acceptable. For the "Egg" of course, large water rudders or fins would have complicated the process of launching down the ramp.

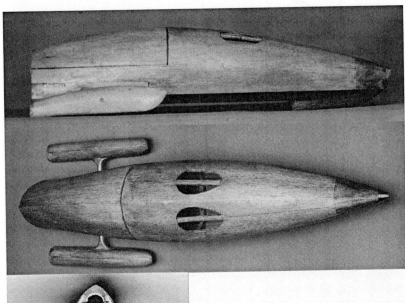

1/16th Scale development model. Probably "E", or early CJK

Vosper

Despite these developments, the achievement of a model which would float at rest, lift itself out of the water, and perform satisfactorily at speed proved at first to be frustratingly elusive.

Towards the ultimate shape.

Because progress towards a satisfactory model which would get over the hump, and reach the desired speed without displaying any instability was proving unexpectedly slow, Railton, unable to be involved with the detailed development whilst in America, was keen to help in any other way that he could.

He had been gathering information on the state of the art in the USA, and in the course of his investigations contacted a friend, Douglas Van Patten, who had designed *Miss Canada*. This boat, in which Du Cane had already expressed an interest, was now showing signs of being able to challenge the water speed record. Railton reported that *Miss Canada* had twice reached 150 m.p.h., but had been unable to complete the required two runs in opposite directions because the propeller blades bent under load.

Because of Vosper's development problems in trying to get their models to start from rest, Railton suggested that Van Patten should be invited to produce a design as a "second string" for Cobb. This would use something like the aerodynamic shape which they had already developed, but employ Van Patten's multi-stepped form for the hydrodynamics.

Du Cane readily agreed to this idea, but meanwhile was beginning to suspect that the inconsistent results he was obtaining with his models were not entirely the fault of Vosper's designs but were due to erratic performance of the Jetex rockets. This turned out to be the case, and there followed a long argument with Wilmot and Mansour, and in turn with I.C.I., who manufactured the charges. Stocks of these held by Vosper and A.E.W. were returned to I.C.I, who commented that A.E.W. must have been keeping theirs in the tank, as they were very wet! This may have been because they were hygroscopic, absorbing atmospheric moisture, and Du Cane replied indignantly that all reasonable precautions had been taken and that if any special instructions as to storage had ever been given, they would have been strictly observed.

With the question of full size propulsion still unresolved, he had been considering liquid fuelled rocket motors, and in October 1949 had written to Frank Halford, commenting that if a suitable rocket motor could be found, it might save a considerable amount of weight and cross sectional area. He asked Halford's opinion on the De Havilland Sprite motor, or possibly the Walther which had been developed in Germany for the Messerschmidt 163 interceptor.

Frank Halford

Halford replied that it might be possible to do something about a Sprite, but was not particularly enthusiastic about this idea, his first reaction being that the duration might be rather too short. The Sprite, designed as a self contained booster unit, currently gave 5,000lb of thrust but only for 11 seconds. The Me 163 unit with larger fuel tanks produced 3,750lb of thrust and used fuel at a rate of 1,200lb per minute, or about sixteen times as much as a turbo-jet engine.

Halford had seen a sketch of one of Du Cane's earlier models and wondered how Du Cane now felt about the project as a whole, since, he remarked, whereas *Blue Bird* had looked something like a boat, this new design was more akin to a wingless seaplane. He commented that in view of the gloomy state of the nation he felt that De Havilland would not be allowed to co-operate on the project unless it could be expected to lead to some practical application. Nevertheless, he offered more advice if Du Cane would let him know what duration would be required.

Du Cane apologised for the appearance of his earlier model and said that the recent merging of aero- and hydro-dynamic requirements had now led to a more normal looking hull. However, he had hitherto had to tackle the problems without regard to any future developments of a practical nature.

He thought that the Me163 unit with enough fuel for one minute's running might be a practical proposition if the all-up weight of the boat could be kept below 4,000lb. Halford replied with more data on sizes and weights which did seem to back Du Cane's assessment, but commented that "fitting a rocket to such a machine seems more appropriate for the day after tomorrow than for serious record breaking, but perhaps I am too old fashioned."

Although Railton later commented that at that rate of consumption the fuel costs per run would become significant, nobody had yet mentioned the safety aspect. The Messerschmidt 163 rocket powered interceptor fighter was spectacular in more ways than one. The fuel was notoriously unstable and dangerous to handle, and there were many accidents due to spontaneous explosions, both on the ground and in the air.

Nevertheless, Du Cane continued to pursue the possibility of rocket propulsion, and he and Railton agreed to keep this aspect very quiet for fear that rivals would "steal" the idea.

Cobb too seems to have expressed concern about the competition in America possibly stealing a march on them, as Du Cane commented to him: "In view of what you said the other day I was perhaps a little quick in accepting Van Patten's offer, but I do not think we need fear he will get any dope from us that would enable him to produce a boat say within 18 months of your venture. Once the idea of using rocket propulsion and the general shape are known, there would of course, be no reason to stop him or anyone else going ahead on these lines."

Du Cane next consulted the Royal Aircraft Establishment at Farnborough, and their Rocket Propulsion Establishment at Wescott, who were very helpful and enthusiastic. He wrote to John Cobb that they were "keen as mustard to help" and were developing a rocket which would "produce bags of thrust for a total weight, including fuel for approximately one minute, of about 1500lb." He added "Please tread very warily about what you say to anybody, as of course it would be fatal if our plans leaked out."

Anticipating that despite the delays a successful 1/16th scale model would eventually emerge, Du Cane was already considering the next step. Bearing in mind his previous experiences with *Blue Bird*, he decided that as an additional check once a satisfactory 1/16th model had been developed, a larger scale model would be advisable before embarking on full size construction. Any tendency to porpoising or other undesirable effects would be more likely to show up, since at a larger scale the Reynolds Number – a function of size and speed which has considerable influence upon the aerodynamic effects – would be much closer to full scale at the model water speeds required by Froude's Law.

The question of propulsion for this larger model arose, and Wescott also offered to help by developing a suitable rocket. There was discussion of a liquid fuelled motor, suitable for a 1/5th, or possibly even larger, scale model, and of a smaller solid fuelled one which would provide about 30lb of thrust needed for a 1/6th scale model.

As the New Year of 1950 dawned, Du Cane was still having problems with the 1/16th scale models. At least part of the trouble was due to the continuing erratic behaviour of the Jetex motors, and although Du Cane never seems to have been too proud to seek or accept suggestions and advice from other people, in this instance he used Van Patten's possible involvement as a stick to beat Wilmot, saying that he was in danger of losing his important client to an American designer because of the inability of Jetex to perform consistently.

Despite this he was still trying experiments with two different models (probably CJK series, versions of "E" and "F", as already discussed). Early in January he wrote to Railton that both performed well when launched from the ramp but still refused to unstick when launched from the water, which, he commented, was precisely what the latter had predicted and what he himself had thought would not be a problem. He had tried various modifications to the nose but so far without success.

Although admitting that this was not as easy as he had thought, he did not regard the problem as insoluble. Nevertheless, he agreed that it would be wise to have the Van Patten alternative up their sleeve.

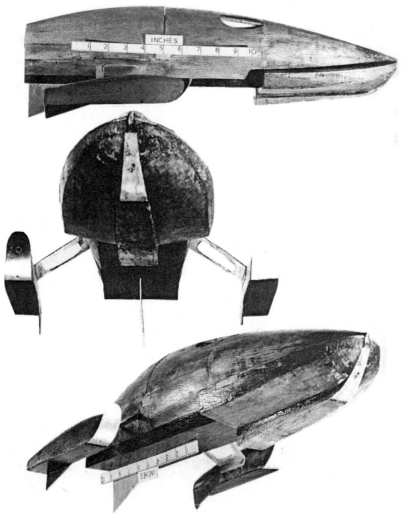

CJK Series 1/16th model. Probably a late version.   AEW/Qinetic

Railton, probably frustrated by being unable to help Du Cane directly, was keen to get on with the Van Patten exercise, which was still in abeyance. He wrote to Cobb, (also sending a copy to Du Cane) that he thought it was "his move" and had therefore had a discussion with Van Patten, specifying limitations of shape and layout imposed by aerodynamic considerations, and asked him to give the project some thought with a view to them jointly producing a design, and probably a 1/16th scale model.

The problem was that there were no suitable test facilities available to them in America, the only possibility being the University of Michigan at Ann Arbor, who had a small tank, reportedly capable of towing at 12 m.p.h. Railton concluded that this would probably be enough to investigate the transition from rest to planing, and that thereafter any model would have to be sent to England for further trials and comparison with the Vosper versions. No equivalent to "Jetex" was available in the U.S.A., and importing the necessary motors from the U.K. would have been too complicated, as the fuel was classed as an explosive.

Meanwhile back in England the Jetex motor reliability problem was eventually solved, and by the end of February 1950 the latest batch of charges seemed to be working satisfactorily, although I.C.I. insisted on charging Wilmot & Mansour £65 for the necessary development work, which cost the latter wanted to pass on to Vosper. This was a lot of money in those days, especially for rectifying a problem which Du Cane believed should not have occurred in the first place, but ruffled feelings all round were finally smoothed down in early April when John Cobb contributed £30 towards this cost.

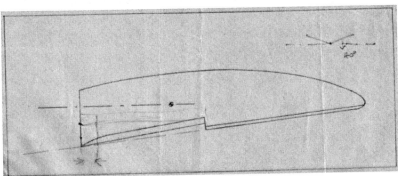

The "Seaplane Float"

Following his discussion during the previous June with Mr. Perring of the R.A.E., Du Cane had been in touch with other experts at Farnborough and, as a result, had sketched an alternative monohull design, rather along the lines of a seaplane float.

Further discussion with R.A.E. led to slight changes to this first sketch, and subsequently Vosper built a model.

By then model trials with the CJK series reverse three point configuration were yielding better results and modifications had led to a model which would "unstick" much more readily. Du Cane wrote to Railton that he was certain that this problem could be solved by drastic changes to the forebody, but he was deliberately progressing by small steps in an endeavour to upset the aerodynamics as little as possible: A shape which produced good hydrodynamic lift at the bow could well lead to a large aerodynamic upward pitching moment at higher speeds. Many modifications were made to the models at this stage.

Du Cane and Railton were exchanging letters and drawings throughout, and most of this correspondence was of course also copied to John Cobb. Some of Du Cane's model photographs had gone astray for a while en route to Railton, who also had to move between Detroit and California, and both men were clearly finding it difficult to exchange up to date details of their respective progress. Letters crossed in the post, and Railton wrote that he didn't think he could make any useful comment at that distance, particularly as he didn't even know the details of the planing surface being used. There were hundreds of questions he wanted to ask, but realised it would just be a waste of time and stationery. Du Cane commented that it was all fearfully difficult to explain and he wished to goodness there was not 5000 miles or so between them. Such problems are difficult to understand nowadays, with communications improved beyond recognition.

As well as news of model development, Du Cane had also tried to keep Railton updated on his investigations into possible rocket propulsion, for the full size as well as for larger models. The Rocket Propulsion Establishment at Westcott were now offering 3500lb of thrust for one minute, but Railton thought that this seemed a bit on the low side to achieve 200 m.p.h. in spite of the low weight and the possibility of a substantial reduction in hull cross section because the rocket would be much smaller than a jet engine.

In order to ease the communication problem Du Cane even considered flying to America at the beginning of February 1950, but soon decided that this was not worthwhile, as he wrote to Railton that probably all he could tell him and Van Patten was a lot of things *not* to do! On the other hand he recognised that Van Patten had recent experience which might be of great value and he was content to await the outcome.

He also wrote to Cobb that in many ways he was happier with things like this, as whilst admitting to having been rather slow in formulating them, he now had some fairly concrete ideas and wanted to iron out his difficulties systematically, dealing with them one by one. He commented that even in the case of the *Blue Bird* there had been an extraordinary number of problems, many of which Railton (who had been frequently in America at that time also) had probably never even been aware.

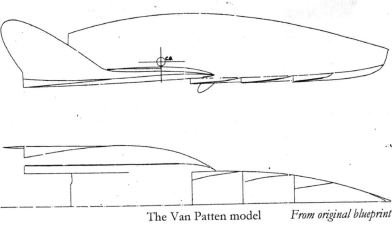

The Van Patten model   *From original blueprint*

A month later he was able to report to Railton that the model rockets were again going well. His latest design was performing satisfactorily and was now at A.E.W. for detailed performance assessment. He wanted to try some further ideas, but thereafter would be ready to get the effect of the latest changes on the aerodynamics checked in the wind tunnel.

Meanwhile Railton and Van Patten had been busy developing their design. They sent a print of it to John Cobb for him to pass on to Du Cane, who duly received it about the end of March together with a letter reporting that they had made a 1/16th scale model and persuaded the University of Michigan to test it.

The University had managed to tune up their carriage to travel at 10 m.p.h. – described as "a record for the course" – which gave a scale speed of 40 m.p.h. This was enough to take their model well over the "hump", at which speed the drag figures were very encouraging, but they had no means of measuring the resistance or observing general behaviour at higher speeds. Railton therefore decided to send the model to Du Cane for further testing at Haslar. He also suggested that a wind tunnel model should be made which could be ready for testing by the time he planned to arrive back in England in June.

Conveniently, John Cobb was visiting the Eastern U.S.A. in early April, so Railton, who was going to be in California, suggested that Van Patten should meet him there, at Cobb's "usual kennel", the Govenor Clinton Hotel, New York, with the model. He added "I particularly hope you will see him and do the civil because he has spent a lot of time on this thing completely f.o.c."

Cobb no doubt did this, and by the end of April he was back home and had delivered the model to Du Cane, along with most comprehensive hand written instructions for its care and maintenance, which explained that it had been finished with a mixture of shellac and mineral oil to provide a smooth and readily renewable standard surface from the viewpoint of the skin friction component of the model's resistance.

Testing it in America had established that with the three step configuration the forebody would unstick readily, although Railton commented that the stern was "rather sticky". He also expressed reservations about its possible resistance at higher speeds, and the effect of the comparatively wide beam forward upon the aerodynamics, which he guessed would be acceptable, but only just. The model only reproduced the lower half, and a streamlined superstructure would have to be built on top for fully representative trials at high speed, but to start with, at least, only the hydrodynamic drag was of interest.

Du Cane commented that in his view water fins were much to be preferred to air fins for directional stability and that he thought that, when yawed, one of the twin fins would be blanketed by the main body. He had arranged with Gawn to have it tested and was looking forward to seeing the results, without which, he wrote, it would be difficult to make further comment. They had agreed that it was not necessary at this stage to add the superstructure, other than a Perspex deck to keep out the water. Unfortunately, Haslar was now very busy and regretted that they could do no more testing for at least a fortnight; until the middle of May

Du Cane was now confident that the latest Vosper version could do the job with just a little more development aimed at improving the unsticking, and sent Railton a photograph of it. He had also demonstrated it to Cobb when the latter had delivered the Van Patten model, and the latter was most impressed with it. This one (probably a derivative of "F") still used exactly the same planing surface configuration as the three legged "Egg", which at high speed Du Cane considered to be the best of the lot, but of course had been unable to hoist itself out of the water.

He was also still considering other models, one of which was the Farnborough "Seaplane Float" option which he had by now tried free running with a Jetex motor. It proved to be quick to unstick, did not porpoise and seemed quite fast, but a little short on transverse stability. Being a monohull, it would be simple and relatively cheap to build. Because free running trials yielded no real quantitative data he asked the R.A.E., who possessed a towing tank of their own, to test this model. Unfortunately the department concerned were heavily occupied and although happy to offer verbal advice were evasive about going any further. They responded by asking him to follow the normal procedure of getting permission from the Ministry "through the official channels", and added that as the Admiralty were more concerned with boats than they were, it might be better if they made the tests, which gave a broad hint as to what the answer would be.

Du Cane gave up at this and at first suggested that they dispose of his model "if it had become an embarrassment to them", but then collected it from them as Haslar expressed an interest in it. However, due to maintenance of the tank or pressure of other work, the latter had still not been able to carry out any further tank tests by the end of May 1950, and regretted that it would still be another fortnight at least before they could do so.

As the "Sea plane float" was effectively a "two point" hull, similar in principle to the first *Blue Bird,* it is difficult to see why it was pursued even this far, except perhaps solely as an attempt to understand the porpoising problem better. Although there is no mention of its aerodynamics, its beam may have proved a disadvantage in this respect. At any rate, there is no further record of this model in the files. Tim Parr, who built most of the 1/16th scale models, remembers a trial in the wet dock with one which had no separate rear sponsons. This, he said, turned out to be a total disaster, as the model turned on its side and then took off! This may have been the swansong of the "Sea plane float", alternatively it may have been version "C", with the integral sponsons, which had proved to be unstable.

Du Cane at his drawing board

Du Cane's thoughts were again turning to larger scale models which would increase confidence that the full size boat would behave in a satisfactory manner. The Rocket Propulsion Department at Wescott were still considering the problem of propelling such a model, and now looked more closely at another solid fuel rocket. It would employ a cigarette-burning coated charge about 5 inches in diameter by 10 inches long, which they calculated would produce a thrust of about 30lb. This would be adequate for a 1/6th scale model, and Du Cane had estimated that if the motor weighed between 8 and 10lb, a model could be built to the correct weight. Westcott commented that if they used standard components the weight would be substantially more than this, but they hoped to be able to keep it down to around 10lb by making some special parts. This later proved difficult.

Plans for a liquid fuelled version suitable for a larger scale model were still being discussed at this stage although Wescott commented that it would "have to be fitted in with other work", and it does not seem to have progressed much further, possibly for this reason, and successful trials later with the 30lb solid rocket – later christened "Water Baby" – rendered it less necessary.

Active consideration was still being given to rocket propulsion for the eventual full sized boat, but in early June, John Cobb found a newspaper article announcing trials on the Clyde using four Derwent jet engines to propel an old paddle steamer *Lucy Ashton*. The purpose was purely experimental, to check actual hull resistance against model test results. Cobb however deduced that "it does not look as if it is too difficult to get the loan of a jet engine." Du Cane attended these trials and managed to find out that these engines had been provided by the Ministry of Supply. Also at the *Lucy Ashton* trial, he met an instrumentation engineer called Macklow-Smith, whose equipment was used to measure the engine thrust, and he bore this in mind for possible future use. The thrust of the "Water Baby" rocket proved to vary considerably and it would be valuable to be able to measure it in order to get a reliable performance assessment.

About this time Cobb asked for a statement of everything he owed Vosper to date, saying he was particularly anxious to keep track of expenditure. Du Cane replied that the cost of the model trials and other investigations had so far been met from Vosper overheads – in other words, Cobb was not charged - but if construction was to commence that would be a different matter.

Around the third week of June Haslar was again able to devote some tank time to Vosper and the first task was probably to carry out comparative towing tests, up to the maximum obtainable equivalent full scale speed of about 95 m.p.h., on the Van Patten model and the two latest Vosper models. These latter were probably descendants of versions designated earlier "E" and "F", referred to by Haslar collectively as "CJK" and by Vosper, rather loosely, as "Vosper I" and "Vosper II" and both also, confusingly, as "Form B", (the "Egg on skis" now being referred to as "Form A")

Graphical records comparing resistances show Railton's previous assessment of the Van Patten model (also referred to by Gawn as the "Railton"!) to be quite correct: It had relatively low resistance at the "hump", but as the maximum speed of the towing carriage approached, its resistance was not only high but increasing rapidly. Resistance of the two Vosper models under similar conditions seemed to be decreasing with increasing speed, but they had much more difficulty in getting over the hump. Comparative figures for *Blue Bird* are included which show that at around 100 m.p.h. it had lower resistance than any of the later models at that time.

Towing trials with "Vosper II" at first produced lower drag figures (better than "Vosper I" but worse than *Blue Bird*) but at the achievable towing speeds results were erratic and Du Cane had trouble reproducing these. He thought that this was probably due to wake from the forward surface interfering with the after part of the main hull. He was sure that this could be improved upon and that this effect would disappear at higher speeds. At this stage, Vosper II was his preferred solution.

Following Reid Railton's arrival in the UK on 1st July for a stay of some two months, he and Du Cane were able spend some time together at Haslar. Because obviously there was no need for written correspondence between them during this period, it is difficult to know exactly what happened, but some conclusions can safely be drawn from graphs of test results and from later correspondence:

Du Cane had already discarded the "Seaplane Float" model, and there is no documentary evidence to show that the Van Patten model was ever tested with a rocket motor for general behaviour at higher speeds. Indeed, this is borne out by the appearance of the model itself which can be seen in the accompanying photographs. The model has lost its third step and part of the undersides of the sponsons; possibly deliberate modifications in an attempt to reduce drag. However, Du Cane later wrote that most of the remainder of the summer of 1950 was spent testing it, and surviving graphical results show that it was certainly towed at several different speeds. It is probable that it was at this stage that they agreed to abandon it too, indeed Railton later wrote that its trials were "disappointing", and Du Cane recorded that it was unsuccessful, at least as far as it went. Efforts thereafter concentrated on improving the Vosper models.

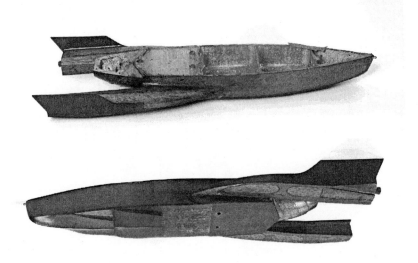

The Van Patten model

AEW/Qinetic

Shortly after Railton's arrival another model was constructed, referred to as "CJQ", (alias "Form C"!) which later went through several variations up to CJQ4. This model had a shortened main hull with about half of the length of the rear sponsons protruding behind it, probably in an attempt to avoid the problem of wake interfering with the after part. Du Cane's notes make it clear that at this stage their main object was to try to improve the unsticking qualities. CJQ2 had the transom partially cut away, which reduced resistance generally, and CJQ3 had the centre of gravity moved well back, which helped at lower speeds but made matters worse the faster it went. CJQ 4 had the width of the forward step reduced to about $1/3^{rd}$ that of its predecessors, removing material from each side. This increased the low speed resistance considerably but the trend indicated that it might then become less than that of the wide step versions at speeds beyond the maximum obtainable in the tank. Most of the graphs of these results which have survived are confusing, partly because it is difficult to identify the actual models concerned, and also because supposed "curves" are constructed from a few points only. Indeed, one graph carries a note to the effect that "points and curves are tendencies only and do not purport to be accurate"! Some, but not all, are corrected for resistance of the towing gear, and in some cases full scale resistance in pounds is plotted whereas others show the ratio of resistance to displacement. All of this complicates meaningful comparison fifty years later.

Model CJQ   *AEW/Qinetiq*

The biggest problem of all was that the maximum full scale speed which could be simulated at $1/16^{th}$ scale was, as ever, limited by the speed of the towing carriage to around 95 m.p.h., whereas the area of interest was from about 150 to 250 m.p.h. Everything depended on the shape of the resistance curves beyond the region which could be explored in any quantitative way. Timing the free running models was tricky, and in any case the rocket thrust was known to vary considerably even over the duration of a single run. In an attempt to explore a higher speed range Du Cane tried towing models with a speedboat, which achieved the full scale equivalent of about 112 m.p.h. Although somewhat rough and ready, this at least demonstrated that the hydrodynamic resistance of the Vosper I and II models did indeed fall with increasing speed, and compared much more favourably with *Blue Bird.* Nevertheless, much still depended on incomplete data backed up by informed guesswork or even hunches!

For such reasons it is difficult to follow the train of development in detail. Trials, and, evidently, further small improvements, continued into mid October 1950, long after Railton had had to return to America, but eventually one model emerged as the favourite, and it was decided, with Cobb's agreement, to use this as the basis for the larger, $1/6^{th}$ scale, version. This seems to have been a close approximation to the longer bodied CJK10, (alias Version "F" and "Form B"!), and it has to be said that, compared to most of the other models, it *looked* right, which according to a well established engineering adage meant that it probably *was* right! Although there are no quantitative trials records to justify this choice it seems likely that the quality of performance of the rocket propelled model confirmed Du Cane's earlier guess that the interference drag from the wake of the forward planing surface did indeed reduce at higher speeds.

At this point, mindful of the still unresolved problem of full sized propulsion, Du Cane sent a photograph of it to Frank Halford, saying that this model offered superior results in every way to *Blue Bird,* and that he thought that at full scale it would achieve something over 200 m.p.h with a "Goblin" engine. He added that Vosper were now making the $1/6^{th}$ scale model which they expected to achieve about 85 m.p.h. He added "I thought I would just let you know what is happening as you appeared to be at least interested personally even though your firm could not do much about it at the time."

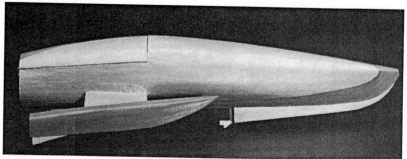

The ultimate shape – almost!   *Vosper*

At the same time he wrote to Cobb, who had suggested that it might now be a good time to talk to De Havilland or Rolls Royce about engines, saying that he had written to Halford but had not asked directly for an engine, as he thought that they ought to wait until the $1/6^{th}$ scale model results were available.

"All the same" he concluded "the story is pretty good."

The fastest model in the world.

On 26th June 1950, whilst Railton was on his way to the UK and Du Cane was busy towing 1/16th models at Haslar, Stanley Sayers in Seattle took the World Water Speed Record at 160.32 m.p.h. in a boat called *Slo-Mo-Shun*, designed by Ted Jones. They then took the boat to Detroit where Jones drove it to win the Gold Cup with ease.

The fact that America had successfully broken Sir Malcolm Campbell's pre-war record hardly came as a shock, but *Slo-Mo-Shun* and her designer were more of a surprise. The boat was an Apel type three pointer, except that at speed the stern was virtually clear of the water and the third "point" was the propeller, half of which was above the surface of the water. This was the "prop rider" configuration which was becoming popular in America and proving to be capable of very high speeds.

With almost all of the hull out of the water, a very large proportion of the drag of a conventional propeller driven boat was due to the drive shaft and its supporting brackets, and thus if most of this, along with the aft step itself, could be lifted out of the water, the reduction in drag more than compensated for the loss of thrust due to the propeller being only partly submerged. Although operating above the "surface", the top half still drew in a good deal of water and generated the characteristic "rooster tail" of spray.

After returning to Detroit in the autumn of 1950, Railton found that the boat and her designer Ted Jones had already gone home to Seattle so he was unable to visit them immediately. However, Van Patten was able to tell him quite a lot about the subject, and Railton himself was able to visit Seattle to meet Jones and examine the boat early in the New Year of 1951. He was therefore able to pass quite a lot of information to Du Cane.

Jones was a pre-flight superintendent at Boeing and boating had been his hobby for many years. He had never done any model testing and *Slo-Mo-Shun* was his first really fast boat. Development had been by trial and error methods; for example, he had found that moving the centre of gravity far enough forwards lifted the propeller half out of the water and gave a lot more speed. He was well aware of the aerodynamic effect, and considered that it was at least partly responsible for the good performance. In fact, he thought that at top speed the front of his boat was nearly airborne and with most of the stern also clear of the water the hydrodynamic drag was very low indeed. He related several instances of the boat leaving the water entirely for considerable distances before crashing back on one sponson, without any serious effect.

Railton commented that the American designer, who did not pretend to be a professional engineer, found it difficult to discuss aerodynamic instability in any more detail. He thought that if Jones was correct the aerodynamics would be critical, and that it was fortunate that the centre of gravity was well forward, or the boat would have flipped onto its back. He concluded that in spite of the American's success, their own design approach to the aerodynamic problem was still the correct one, and moreover that nobody would be able to reach 200 m.p.h. with a water propeller. He was certainly not far from the truth on both counts because although *Slo-Mo-Shun* still had more successes to come, her eventual best speed was around 180, and she was finally to be badly damaged when flipping over after striking a wake.

Nevertheless he and Du Cane were impressed with the achievements of this gifted "amateur". Railton commented that he found it "humiliating!" (although his exclamation mark indicated that he took it in good part) and Du Cane remarked sarcastically that "it just shows you what a technical education does!"

Meanwhile back at Vospers in December 1950, the 1/6th scale model was under construction. John Cobb had authorised the building of two hulls, but it is not clear whether both were actually built as the original plan appears to have been to try both the short (CJQ) form and the longer version developed from the CJK series. In fact, only the latter seems to have been tested, and was damaged and rebuilt several times, with different sponsons, forward planing surfaces, and cantilever support arrangements.

R.P.E. Wescott had developed the "Water Baby" solid fuel rocket to propel it. This was similar in principle to the Jetex rockets but much larger. The design thrust was 30lb, but R.P.E. had difficulty in keeping this reasonably constant and early trial firings showed that that it might vary between 20 and 40lb over its 20 second running time. As with the smaller free running models it was very difficult or impossible to measure acceleration or speed reliably, and this widely variable thrust made accurate performance analysis even more difficult.

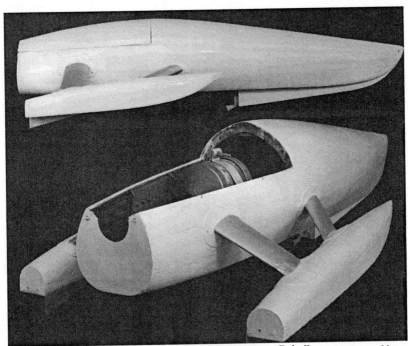

One sixth scale model with "Water Baby".   *Vosper*

It was at first stipulated that refuelling of the rocket cases had to be done at Wescott, and this therefore limited the number of possible runs on each occasion to the available number of motor cases. Du Cane therefore was keen to have as many cases as possible available, as returning them to Wescott each time would have been very time consuming. Probably for this reason the rules were quickly changed so that Wescott personnel could refill them and fire them on site, and only two motor cases were necessary. Later on it seems that rules were relaxed further so that recharging and firing, which was done electrically, could be done by Vosper personnel.

Although the main purpose of the rocket driven models was the assessment of stability and general behaviour, it was also highly desirable to obtain some idea of drag figures in the speed range beyond that which could be achieved by the towing carriage. Du Cane made enquiries about a suitable thrust recorder from Macklow-Smith, whom he had met during the *Lucy*

Ashton trial in Scotland, and although the latter could offer a sensor, and expressed interest in eventually instrumenting the full sized boat, he was unable to provide a suitable recorder. Much later in the 1/6th model trials programme, RAE devised a suitable system but meanwhile thrust and therefore drag could only be guessed.

Preliminary estimates were that the model would weigh around 30lb and achieve a speed of about 85 m.p.h. The question of safety obviously arose; in those days there was no reliable radio control equipment available which was small and light enough to be carried in the model. AEW had a gyroscopic control system which could, in theory, at least keep the model on a straight course but were struggling to keep the weight of this equipment down to below 6 pounds.

The first runs of this model were carried out at AEW's Horsea torpedo range, a long, straight lake surrounded by steep banks next to the upper reaches of Portsmouth Harbour, opposite Vosper's Portchester Shipyard. During the first attempt on 24th January 1951, the water was rough and the model bucked badly. The next day however was a complete success, and the model was timed at 97.5 m.p.h, and estimated to be still accelerating until the rocket burned out, when it came to rest unharmed. Gawn commented that with just a little more effort they might have beaten the new American record with a six foot model!

97.5 m.p.h!   *AEW/Qinetiq*

Du Cane immediately wrote to Railton with news of this successful trial, and although the letter was sent to California when Railton was apparently on his way to Detroit, Jean Carpenter sent a second copy which reached him by February 3rd, when he wrote back full of praise, enthusiasm, and ideas.

He considered the trial to have been "historic", and that Du Cane's efforts in working up the model were "beyond praise." He concluded that if they could get hold of an engine to produce 7,000lb of thrust, and keep the displacement down to 6,500lb, they could doubtless now build a boat capable of at least 225 m.p.h. and possibly as much as 250. This, he commented, was close to the target they had set two years before, except that they had hoped to keep the necessary thrust down to 4,500lb. (In fact, Railton had originally said that it would be foolish to aim at less than 200 m.p.h., which meant designing for aerodynamic safety up to at least 250.)

The displacement of the model was estimated to be around 31½lb, the equivalent of which was higher than they hoped to achieve at full scale, but the model was somewhat overweight on account of the rocket motor and the gyroscopic steering gear. However, the thrust of the rocket, estimated to average about 32lb, was also on the high side and the thrust to displacement ratio was about right.

Based on this information, Railton had done some calculations. They had a good estimate of the aerodynamic resistance from the wind tunnel results, and the thrust was known. They also had reasonable estimates of the resistances of *Blue Bird* and *Slo-Mo-Shun* for comparison, and so he concluded that the hydrodynamic resistance of the new model still seemed very high. He suggested several reasons for this, namely; possible interference between the forward and aft planing surfaces, (as Du Cane already suspected at lower speeds); the lack of the aerodynamic lift which they had carefully reduced, and which therefore did nothing to reduce the effective displacement; the possibility that hydrodynamic drag increased with speed; and finally the possibility that nose down pitching moment due to the jet thrust actually increased the effective displacement.

He concluded that, on the basis of the current model results, a full size boat weighing 6,000lb would need between 5,500 and 6,000lb of thrust to succeed, and that therefore something more needed to be done to reduce the hydrodynamic drag.

He suggested that perhaps the optimum angle of attack of the planing surfaces might reduce as the speed increased. With the three-point layout, this angle was virtually fixed once the boat was planing, and the optimum angle for getting over the hump and for general performance thereafter had already been determined after many trials. He suggested however that if the profile of the back of the planing surfaces, viewed from the side, was made slightly circular, so that the angle of attack reduced at the trailing edges, then although the effective angle at low speeds would be virtually unaltered, at high speeds when the boat rose further out of the water, the angle would be reduced.

He also suggested that further runs be made at reduced thrust, in order to establish more points on the curve of resistance against speed, and requested more data on timing and positions of the model during the run, variation of thrust with speed, and various drawings. If sufficient data were available this should enable better estimates to be made of speed, acceleration, thrust and therefore resistance at various different points on the run.

Du Cane wrote back at some length but although he too would have liked the data which Railton requested, it simply was not available owing to the difficulty of measuring the various parameters during the run. He did not agree with Railton that some major source of hydrodynamic drag remained to be eliminated, because he considered that the low hydrodynamic drag of other hulls was due to the effect of aerodynamic lift. Perhaps some small improvements might yet result from further model tests. He was less pessimistic than Railton about the potential performance of the full size and cautioned against drawing too many conclusions from the rather sketchy numerical data available. The main objective of the free running model was to check qualitative performance – stability – rather than to collect quantitative data, which was difficult with the available facilities. Nevertheless he wrote to Cobb that although it might yet take months to produce an accurate estimate of full scale speed performance, his own estimate was now approximately 220 m.p.h., and he reminded Cobb that although they all now seemed to be contemplating 250, the original target had been 200.

He tried Railton's idea relating to the profile of the planing surfaces on a 1/16th scale model and reported that it had behaved well, although made no comment on its effect on performance, presumably because of the usual difficulty of measuring speed accurately.

The success of the run on January 25th prompted Du Cane to organise a demonstration for several important people, including Gawn of A.E.W., Dr. Cawood of Wescott, and Frank Halford from De Havilland. Not surprisingly, on 21st February the weather was unsuitable, but nevertheless an attempt was made rather than to disappoint the spectators. In choppy conditions and a force 3 to 4 crosswind, the model ran for 200 yards and then reared up and turned over, doing some damage to itself.

However, this attempt, although unsuccessful, was regarded as very sporting in the circumstances and certainly did the project no harm. Shortly afterwards Du Cane was able to report to Railton that there now almost seemed to be competition between De Havilland and Wescott as to who could provide the motive power for the full size boat: Halford thought that he would be able to arrange the loan of a "Ghost" which produced 5,300lb of static thrust, and some 4,900 at about 230 m.p.h.

Railton wrote that he thought he should be present at this crucial stage, and Du Cane welcomed the news that he had booked aboard the *Queen Mary* to arrive in England on 5th April, 1951.

Gawn came up with some provisional estimates of full size performance based on the model runs. These seem to amount simply to scaling up speed from 97 m.p.h. using the square root law, resulting in 238 m.ph., and scaling up displacement by the cube of the scale, resulting in the 31.5lb model becoming 6,800lb., and requiring 6910lb of thrust.

At first sight, this was discouraging, and Du Cane agreed that on that basis there was apparently not much chance of achieving 250 m.p.h. with 5,000lb of thrust, but pointed out that everyone seemed to have again forgotten that the original target had been 200. Also that the latest estimate was that the "Water Baby" thrust during the run had only been 30lb, not 32, which helped somewhat. He considered that the all up weight of the full size should be around 5,500lb, and although this eventually turned out to be optimistic, there were certainly gains to be made here too. He wrote to Gawn that he was loath to get pinned down on performance predictions from the 1/6th scale runs at this stage, as the primary objective was demonstration of satisfactory behaviour.

In an attempt to obtain more quantitative data from the rocket propelled model runs Westcott had agreed to modify "Water Baby" to produce a reduced thrust of 25lb, and were also working on a means of recording thrust during the run. They sent a sketch of a modified venturi plate for the "Water Baby", suggesting that Vosper made one and sent it back to them with a motor case for test firing. For thrust measurement, they had considered "crusher" gauges, by which parts of the engine mount would be permanently compressed if the thrust exceeded certain values, but concluded that it was not feasible in this case. Instead they were devising a simple gauge to register peak pressure inside the motor, from which thrust could be estimated. Du Cane replied by suggesting that perhaps it could be made to record throughout the run by using a small circular chart driven by a stopwatch.

He was also wondering about the validity of full size speed predictions from the model results, using Froude's square root law, since this was generally used for displacement craft and they were now into unexplored territory with planing models which only touched the water in small spots. He posed this question to several experts including Gawn, and others at the Director of Naval Construction's Department at Whitehall. This generated several lengthy technical letters, the general consensus amongst the Naval Architects being that the Froude law was valid, although suitable corrections had to be made for friction drag of the water as well as the air. Mike Hooper, the aerodynamicist from Fairey, was less certain. After a further lengthy technical discussion he suggested changes to the planing angles to try to reduce drag, which Du Cane was most reluctant to do for fear of upsetting the stability again. All concerned seemed to agree on the difficulty of calculating the frictional components of drag, which were obviously significant, and extrapolating them to full size.

All of this only serves to emphasise the difficulty of obtaining accurate quantitative performance predictions with the technology of the time. Du Cane commented to Halford that although there did not seem to be any reasonable doubt whatsoever that the general behaviour was satisfactory, there was still room for debate on performance as nobody seemed able to make confident full scale predictions from model tests. Those best qualified to do so, he continued, now gave predictions varying between 200 and 230 m.p.h. for 4750lb of jet thrust. His own guess was 220 m.p.h. with the current model design.

Wescott had meanwhile carried out three successful trial firings with the motor modified for reduced thrust and returned it to Vosper ready for use. This happily coincided with Railton's arrival in the UK and he was present at a model run at Horsea on 9th April 1951, when the reduced thrust was tried for the first time.

The files contain two, originally identical, carbon copies of a "diary" of 1/6th model runs, typed in spreadsheet form, recording the dates, conditions and results of each run. One copy has been amended in Du Cane's handwriting, and the second copy, which lacks these amendments, has obviously been added to later to include details of several additional runs. On the whole, it is possible to correlate these with remarks in the correspondence, but there remain a few gaps and inconsistencies.

For example, there appears to have been confusion between the 9th April run, and the following one on 25th April, possibly due to confusion on the part of the typist when transcribing cryptic handwritten notes onto a large complicated table, and these are the records amended later by Du Cane. The most likely interpretation is that on the 9th April, in Du Cane's words, "the model planed well but steering gear was obviously erratic and overcorrected several times, causing excessive yaw and eventual overturning." Speed was estimated as 93 m.p.h. with the reduced thrust at 26lb.

After repairs to the model, the next attempt was made at Horsea on the evening of 25th April and was a flop, as the model was scarcely able to leave its dock, let alone get up and plane. Du Cane has written on the record "failure to plane due to forward rudder being hard over, two attempts." This fact was apparently only discovered after the motor was returned to Wescott for checking, the first reaction being, as Du Cane wrote to Westcott, that "either the thrust was considerably lower than it should have been, or the model just would not take it at that thrust."

There was still no means of checking thrust during a run. In early May Wescott sent down their thrust recorder, apparently in an unfinished state, to see whether it would fit in the model. Du Cane sent it back saying that it was excellent, and had been offered up with no difficulty. Although he continued to enquire anxiously as to its progress at regular intervals, it was not ready for use until September.

After the 25th April run, Wescott apparently found nothing wrong with the rocket, and further investigation only then pointed to problems with the steering gear. The "diary" records that the aft rudder was changed to a forward rudder during repairs after 9th April run, but this is probably an error, as in a letter to Gawn on 10th April Du Cane says that it was changed during the major repairs following the 21st February, because it simplified installation and this provided a good opportunity to try it in the model. This letter indicates that Gawn was concerned about the forward rudder configuration, perhaps suggesting that it had been responsible for the erratic run on 9th April. Nevertheless it seems that a problem was found with the gyroscopic control system because Haslar then put in a larger battery, which increased the weight by a pound.

Perhaps because of more troubles with the gyroscopic control, or in order to save weight, the steering gear and rudder were removed at some time during the summer at the beginning of August. This reduced the weight to about 28lb, and the motor was moved forward two inches to correct the trim. Future running relied on fixed fins aft to keep the model straight. This seems to have been successful but of course neither method was able to take avoiding action when posts, mud banks and so on got in the way, and so the model continued to be damaged regularly.

The next run recorded in the "diary" is not until 20th September, probably because of the summer holiday period, but references in correspondence infer that several more were carried out between the end of April and 23rd June, the day Railton was again due to return to America. In a letter to Wescott dated 29th May, Du Cane reported "a fairly successful run the other day", when the model was again damaged, and he again mentioned that he would be pleased to have the thrust recorder when the hull had been repaired. The Waterbaby rocket was possibly still giving cause for concern, as he returned a motor to Westcott a few days later, saying that it had burned for 15 seconds before going out of sight ashore.

Railton's final visit to Portchester before returning to the USA was on 20th June, when Du Cane had promised to lay on "an interesting rig test" and a film of the most recent model run. There are no more details of what the rig test comprised, but the following day Du Cane told Gawn that he thought it almost certain that construction of the full size boat would go ahead. He wrote a similar message to Wescott a few days later, so it was probable that he, Railton and Cobb had come to this conclusion on 20th.

There were still unsolved problems which required further model tests to resolve them. Firstly, the position of the forward cantilever arms supporting the sponsons would be at the position of maximum jet turbine diameter in the full scale, which would pose a severe structural problem. Moving them to a different position might cause hydrodynamic drag problems in getting over the "hump", so the model was modified to test this.

Secondly, both Railton and Du Cane had doubts about the entirely flat undersurface of the sponsons. Running had hitherto concentrated on a narrow forward step and flat bottomed sponsons which were able to get over the hump and worked well at high speed. Experiments with vee shaped surfaces had not so far been successful but on his return to America Railton wrote as a "final word" that he would prefer to risk initial troubles and alterations with the full size than to put up with the possible effect of shock loading on the flat surfaces. He favoured taking a chance and Vee-ing them even if model results were "inconclusive". Du Cane replied that he saw no problem in doing this and was working on it.

He first tried towing the 1/6th model with different configurations of planing surfaces to establish the effects at around the hump speed. In conjunction with the narrow forward step, veed sponsons caused the resistance to rise considerably and the model rolled violently. Substituting a wide forward step with the veed sponsons produced a successful result in the towing tank, and so it was then tried with the high thrust rocket for behaviour at speed. This trial was from Vosper's barge off Portchester, on 20th September, with fixed fins for directional stability, and Du Cane's first reaction was that it was surprisingly successful, despite the fact that the model took off after about 200 yards, as he thought this was probably due to the rough water conditions. But on repeating the trial in calmer water a week later, the same thing happened, which he decided was more than he could safely overlook, and concluded that the wide step generated too much lift, both hydro- and aero-dynamically.

As the full size construction programme would soon necessitate a final decision, he could see no alternative but to return to the narrow forward step and flat sponsons. He wrote to Railton explaining this and asking for his "sympathy and agreement" with this. They had successfully tested a different layout incorporating lower cantilever arms and he remarked that therefore the structural design of these to withstand the expected shock loads would be easier.

Railton replied agreeing that it would be prudent to go ahead with the narrow, flat surfaces, but still finding it inconceivable that these would eventually prove to be the best solution, and commenting that doubtless the flat surfaces would be received with derision by others. He also remarked that, based on the wind tunnel results, the model should not have "taken off". Du Cane agreed with this, saying that he had earlier consulted Hooper of Faireys, who could see no reason why the aerodynamics should have changed greatly. Du Cane was disappointed at not being able to incorporate the vee and was convinced that given time something could be done about this. He considered that the problem might indeed be water conditions and would do some more testing shortly, but meanwhile Cobb wanted no delay to the construction and these two similar mishaps could not be ignored.

The accompanying pictures taken from a film of the model "flying" at Horsea are possibly of the second of these incidents, as the first definitely took place at Portchester. The model in the pictures has a wide front step, no rudder control and (probably) flat bottomed sponsons, in accordance with the "diary" record for the run on 28th September. However, this record also records "low" cantilever arms and the film seems to show high ones. This diary entry could of course be in error.

1/6th Model run with wide step

AEW/Qinetiq

At this point further model testing was hampered by problems with the Waterbaby rocket. Two attempts on 24th October with the reduced thrust version both failed to get over the hump, and Du Cane wrote to Wescott that there had been at least five occasions when the thrust had been far below normal, although in one case it had suddenly recovered.

The next recorded occurrence of this problem with the Waterbaby was on 14th November; perhaps no further runs had been made in the meantime. This time the thrust recorder was in use and two small record charts were sent to Wescott. These were returned, and have survived, but the original trace has almost completely faded. The problem was confined to the low thrust configuration; one firing with the high thrust venturi gave normal good performance. Some four weeks later Wescott wrote back, having concluded that the erratic performance was due to the motor pressure being in the region of unstable burning. The only sure cure would have been to redesign the charge, which would be expensive, so they suggested using only the high thrust venturi in future.

Vospers were by then very busy on detailed design of the boat itself, and ordering materials. In connection with this part of the exercise – which will be covered in the next chapter – Railton paid another visit to the UK for the month of November 1951. He and Du Cane appear to have concentrated on structural calculations rather than model testing during this period, and because Railton seems to have spent much of it away from Portchester, several notes on this topic were exchanged between them. He sailed back to America on 30th November.

Running of the 1/6th scale model continued into 1952, mainly with the object of assessing shock loadings on the structure. This necessitated use of an accelerometer, and an instrument was borrowed from Saunders Roe on the Isle of Wight, who at that time were preparing their huge Princess flying boat prototype for its first flight.

This accelerometer consisted of a series of steel balls held in place at various distances from a magnet, in such a way that each ball would be displaced by a different level of acceleration. Thus after a run, the ball of the highest "value" which had been dislodged would give an indication of the maximum acceleration or shock load which had been experienced.

Some trials with this instrument aboard were carried out at the end of January 1952. The model apparently performed correctly but the accelerometer did not; some of the balls were displaced but others, representing lower accelerations, remained in place, which, as Du Cane commented, was rather difficult to understand! The runs were not wasted as Cobb, his friend

George Eyston of Wakefield Oil, and others witnessed them, and Du Cane wrote to Railton that "all appeared to enjoy themselves quite a lot." Model runs were obviously a good P.R. exercise!

Peter Crewe of Saunders Roe replied that the accelerometer failure was due to dampness, and commented that in view of this further trials would probably be of interest: He would therefore have the accelerometer serviced, recalibrated and waterproofed before returning it.

During the next trial on 13th February the model went so well that it unfortunately ran ashore after ¾ mile, and on hitting the beach flew 8 feet in the air and pitched into a mud bank. It was some consolation that, before doing so, the run was perfect, and that although the accelerometer recorded in excess of 12g, the cantilever arms were slightly distorted on one side only, although the structure in the model was "nothing special". Du Cane had by now also established that the forward rudder worked as expected.

Some final runs on 19th March in rough water recorded accelerations between 5 and 8g. This may have been due to the fact that the model touched a mudbank at some stage, nevertheless it was concluded that the structure, which was calculated to fail at 5g when statically loaded, could stand much higher transient shocks.

These were the final runs of the 1/6th model, and were witnessed by John Cobb and Hawkes, the installation engineer from De Havilland who was becoming increasingly involved in the construction of the new boat.

Du Cane decided that an accelerometer should be installed in the full sized boat and began searching for a suitable instrument. He located one at the Marine Aircraft Experimental Establishment at Felixstowe, and the Superintendent agreed to lend it to them, subject to availability at the time of the full size trials. As anticipated, this gentleman suggested that the flat planing surfaces might cause what he called high speed "pattering or bouncing". Du Cane replied that this form had run in a reliable and stable manner, and although later model runs had achieved a satisfactory alternative form, it was by then too late to modify the full size boat.

It is unfortunately not clear which this alternative form was; presumably it incorporated some "Vee" but whether it would have needed more width forward than would have been aerodynamically acceptable is not known.

At Railton's insistence, one final test of the 1/6th model remained to be done. This was to add cockpit, windscreen and air intakes and test it in the wind tunnel once more. Du Cane agreed with this and had already discussed the aerodynamics with Hooper, but as Fairey's wind tunnel was very busy their Managing Director had already "warned Du Cane off", so that the latter was reluctant to press too hard, saying that he believed Hooper, if left to his own devices, would be able manage something, which eventually he did. The model in its final form was sent to him for visual examination and comment on 26th March, and because space in the tunnel was still unavailable was sent back to Vospers on 22nd May. However, it returned to Faireys on 4th June as Hooper obviously saw a possible opportunity coming up, and suggested Du Cane should write to the Chief Engineer, R.L. Lickley, again requesting permission. Whilst awaiting this, the model was taken to C.C. Wakefields, makers of Castrol Oil, and Cobb's sponsors, for some publicity photographs. It returned to Fairey's on 18th June and was tested in early July. Following summer holidays, it finally arrived back at Portchester in mid August.

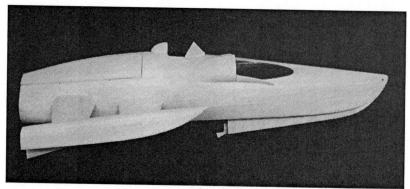

The final model   *Vosper*

Hooper's report shows that because of the necessary modifications to the original model which had been tested in 1949, the aerodynamics had deteriorated. He concluded that at 250 m.p.h. the aerodynamic lift would exceed the weight at around 5 degrees of pitch, and the nose up pitching moment would be enough to overcome the boats weight at about 4 degrees. Alarming conclusions at first sight, but 4 degrees of pitch would have meant the forward step rising nearly a foot from the water whilst the tails of the sponsons remained on the surface, which would have been a very large angle. Moreover, no account was taken of the nose down pitching moment due to the jet engine. Thus in the worst case of a total thrust failure at 250 m.p.h. the boat would still have to be pitched up quite severely by some disturbance before somersaulting.

This was evidently deemed to be acceptable, and the emphasis now shifted entirely to full size design and construction, which had been proceeding apace already since mid 1951 and will now be dealt with in more detail.

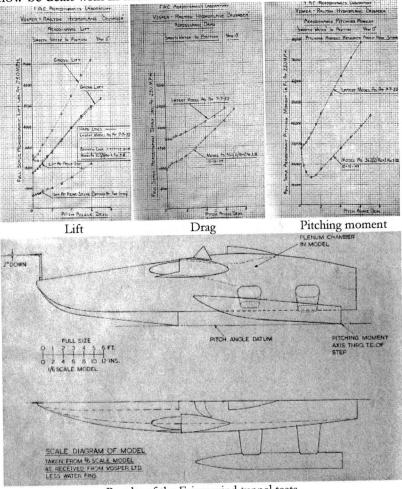

| Lift | Drag | Pitching moment |

Results of the Fairey wind tunnel tests

Theory into practice.

The design of any complex engineering project is usually a compromise between conflicting requirements, and this was inevitably true in the case of John Cobb's boat. The eventual outcome of the model testing had led to a shape which was a compromise between ideal aerodynamic and hydrodynamic characteristics, and had to balance top speed performance with stability, and the ability to get over the hump and later return safely to rest. The various configurations of other extreme fast boats emphasise that there is no one ideal solution to this problem. Cobb's boat pioneered the reverse three pointer layout, and this was adopted by a number of subsequent designs which had their fair share of success as well as disaster. Railton's and Du Cane's painstaking research was on the right track, although their boat was never able to demonstrate its full potential.

When turning from the hydro- and aero-dynamic requirements to the structural design of such a craft, compromise still rules. Extra strength usually means extra weight, and it must be obvious, especially to anyone who has read the chapters on model testing, that weight is all important, each extra pound (or kilogram!) requiring extra thrust from the engine to propel it unless a corresponding reduction in performance is to result. On the other hand, the faster the craft travels, the higher are the loads exerted upon it by the surrounding air and water; these generally increase as the square of the speed: For example, the dynamic pressures on a boat travelling in calm conditions at around 200 m.p.h. would be about twice those experienced at 140 m.p.h., and at 240 m.p.h. some three times the latter. Forces on this boat might therefore be expected to be up to two hundred per cent greater than those experienced by *Blue Bird* in 1939.

This is not a difficult calculation to make, but what is much more difficult is to estimate the effect of transient disturbances such as wave impacts. Obviously, it would be unreasonable to expect a boat such as this to perform in rough water, but on the other hand, equally unreasonable to expect conditions always to be glassy calm. What therefore would be a "reasonable" design condition? And what resulting loads would it impose on the structure, where, and for how long? The model experiments had already suggested that much higher transient

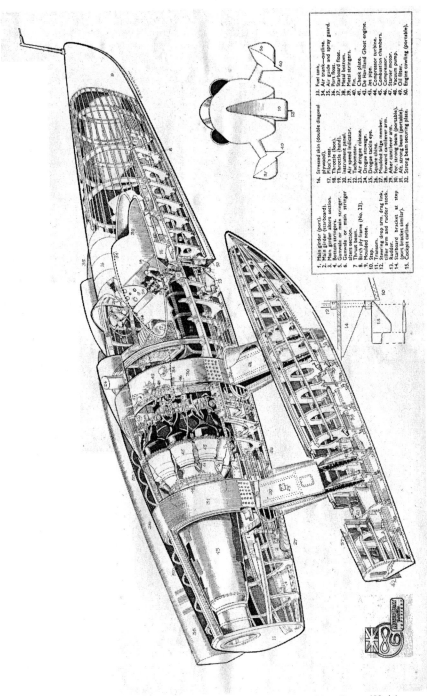

Motor Boat and Yachting.

shocks could be withstood than the same magnitude of steady loading, but how much higher? Data obtained from the accelerometer fitted to the model had been very limited.

Finally, even if realistic conditions could be defined, how could the structure be designed to be strong enough (and, for weight reasons, only just strong enough) to withstand them? The calculation of stresses in such complex structures is not easy, and in 1951, although this science was well advanced, all calculations had to be performed by hand – or at best, by mechanical calculating machines with a fraction of the power of even the most modest modern computer.

There were other factors at work as well, cost being, as ever, prominent amongst them. Cobb was a rich man, but despite the eventual loan of the engine and many of the materials and services required being provided free or at reduced cost, the price tag was frighteningly high. He commented at least once that if he had realised in advance how high it would be, he might never have embarked upon the project. Although there is no suggestion that "cheap" options (implying those of dubious suitability) were adopted in the construction, there was certainly pressure, for other reasons as well as cost, to curtail the programme by reducing the full size trial period to the absolute minimum, and this had a significant bearing on the outcome. So also did the necessity of freezing the design in late 1951 whilst attempts were still being made to devise a suitable configuration of "veed" planing surfaces.

A further problem was the availability of the necessary materials. Many items were in short supply, or unobtainable. For example, problems in obtaining suitable fastenings for the proposed birch ply forward planing surface to some extent influenced the change to aluminium, which was to prove of great significance. Thus achievement of a satisfactory design was not only a difficult technical problem, but was also influenced by several other considerations of a non technical nature.

All of this is not to suggest that the design task was impossible, but it was exceedingly difficult, especially as the boat was an entirely new design and expected to perform well in excess of any previous one. There was an unavoidable element of the unknown, inevitably necessitating a degree of trial and error, which despite the best efforts of Du Cane and Railton, assisted by some of the best available contemporary advice, was always going to result in some risk.

Before even beginning the design task, a firm decision on the type of engine was obviously essential. The choice had long been narrowed down to either rocket or jet reaction propulsion, and each had their advantages and disadvantages. A rocket engine would have been smaller in diameter than a turbojet, offering a smaller cross section and thus less air drag and probably a smaller, and therefore cheaper, boat. The endurance required being only between 20 and 30 seconds for each run meant that the combined weight of motor and fuel was also less than the equivalent for a turbojet, although, because of the prodigious fuel consumption of the rocket, this balance would quickly tip the other way if more than about one minute's endurance was required.

Du Cane was clearly attracted to this solution and Westcott were enthusiastic and helpful. However, they were forced to admit that they would not be able to produce a 6,000lb. thrust rocket for about two years. Two motors of 3,000lb thrust each was a possibility, but somebody raised the question of what might happen if one of them failed at speed, leaving the boat with a sudden dramatic change to the line of thrust. Du Cane thought that perhaps a single 3,000lb. rocket might suffice because its cross sectional area would allow the boat itself to be reduced in size and weight (and indeed, cost); an option which was not open to the larger diameter turbojet. However, Cobb, who was not unsupportive of the rocket option on technical grounds, pointed out that C.C.Wakefield, the makers of "Castrol", and his major sponsor, would have no application for their product in a rocket motor, which would undoubtedly influence their enthusiasm.

Tentative approaches to De Havilland had reopened in October 1950 and the successful 1/6th model trials in early 1951 had helped Halford to persuade his Board to consider more favourably the possibility of providing a turbojet, this time the more modern Ghost rather than a Goblin. As this would mean borrowing one destined for the Ministry of Supply (M.o.S.), the latter would also have to grant their approval, but in the prevailing atmosphere of rearmament in the face of real or imagined threats from the USSR, neither this, nor even the government permission required by Vospers, to obtain the other necessary materials and to divert their own efforts to the building of the boat, would be quick or easy to obtain. However, in February 1951 Cobb visited the new Director (Air) at the M.o.S., Air Marshall John Boothman. Cobb had known him in 1931 when, as a Flight Lieutenant, Boothman had won the Schneider Trophy flying the Supermarine S6B seaplane. The Air Marshall immediately wrote to Halford in support of the water speed project. "I think", wrote Cobb to Railton "this has done the trick."

Thus by the end of February 1951 Halford was much more optimistic about the possibility of eventually solving the political problem. However, he quoted the maximum thrust obtainable from a standard Ghost at 230 m.p.h. as only 4,700lb, which might be increased slightly in view of the short duration required. Some further significant improvement might be obtained by using water injection or reheat but both these methods had drawbacks.

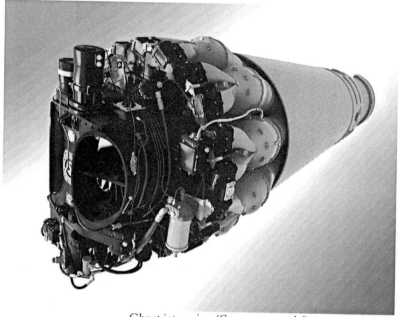

Ghost jet engine (Computer model)   *Architech*

There is no clear indication of when the decision to drop the rocket solution and concentrate on the Ghost was taken, possibly because despite the above mentioned problems with the former, the supply of the latter remained uncertain until late July 1951 and Du Cane was anxious to try to retain the option of a "second string". Also because his debate with RAE, AEW, and Hooper of Fairey Aviation concerning the conclusions about full scale drag and speed predictions to be deduced from the model results (which were themselves subject to measurement errors) continued for some time. This may have cast some doubt on the adequacy of the turbojet performance, although even the most pessimistic estimates were comfortably in excess of the current record, and a 6,000lb. version of the Ghost was under development.

Nevertheless, by mid April 1951 there was at least a tacit understanding that the turbojet was the preferred solution and Halford suggested that he sent an engineer down to Vospers to begin looking at the installation problems. Drawing had started by then but had not progressed far, and Du Cane suggested they be allowed to get a little further with the construction plans before looking more closely at the integration of the engine. Meanwhile, at the beginning of April, Railton had arrived from the USA for one of his visits.

Although there may seem to have been little point in starting on the design unless it was clear that the necessary propulsion unit would indeed be forthcoming, it would have been difficult to approach Boothman, of M.o.S., until they knew clearly what was required, when, and for how long. Similar considerations applied to obtaining the necessary licence to build the boat: Expenditure of scarce material and labour resources which might be required for the rearmament programme was strictly controlled. At the beginning of May Halford seems to have been reasonably confident that the Ministry would cooperate as far as the engine was concerned. He assumed that no significant modifications to the standard Ghost would be required but decided that it would be best not to approach Boothman officially for the time being.

At this stage, before anyone really knew what would be required or how it was to be built, attempts to estimate the cost were even more difficult than the design problem. Nevertheless, at Du Cane's request, John Rix (later Sir John, and successor to Du Cane as Managing Director) attempted the impossible and as a first guess suggested that it would cost roughly three times what

Blue Bird had before the war, due to increased costs and a more complex design. This amounted to about £7,000 for the basic materials and labour alone, without any allowances for overheads, trials, transport, or profit, and based on the assumption that the engine would be loaned free of charge. This figure turned out to be less than half the eventual cost on a similar basis, which goes to show how very difficult estimating such things can be, especially when almost nothing is known about the subject except its size and shape!

Du Cane was well aware of this and has written on the estimate "quoted £15,000 approx." Even this figure was less than the eventual sum, but considering that when it was quoted Vosper was still deeply involved in model trials and were not in any position to make an accurate estimate, it was not a bad guess. Of course, no attempt should be made to compare the actual figures with modern day prices, which have inflated by several orders of magnitude!

Halford had intimated that although the loan of the engine would be free of charge, any necessary modifications would have to be paid for, and in response Du Cane said that he and Cobb had come to a private agreement that Vosper would share the costs of the venture 50/50 with him. Therefore De Havilland could look to Vosper for any such payments. In return for this agreement Cobb would allow Vosper to test the boat in complete privacy before any announcements concerning attempts on the record were made to the media. Clearly this condition was as a result of their unfortunate experiences with *Blue Bird*, and Du Cane knew that Halford would thoroughly approve.

For some reason, Cobb evidently had second thoughts about this arrangement, although he too would certainly have been averse to any premature publicity. On 16th May he discussed it over the phone with Du Cane, who next day wrote to him expressing regret that the proposal did not seem on the whole acceptable to Cobb, and would therefore have to be regretfully withdrawn. "As you know", he wrote "It was put forward as a means of showing our own faith in the scheme and for cutting down the delay as far as possible. "

By the last week in June Du Cane decided that the construction drawings were far enough advanced to make a visit from a De Havilland engineer worthwhile, and by this time more encouraging conclusions were emerging from the continuing model tests and the debate about speed predictions from them. It now seemed certain that the project would go ahead, and Du Cane and Cobb discussed putting the arrangements for this on a slightly more formal footing. This was in the form of a letter, drafted by Du Cane and agreed by the Vosper Board, which Du Cane sent to Cobb for his approval, saying that he thought that before finalising it they perhaps should wait for some definite statement from De Havillands concerning the engine. Cobb agreed, made some small changes to the letter, and sent it back, saying he would sign when Du Cane was ready. He added that he was sure that Du Cane already realised that the venture was a sporting gamble rather than a financial proposition, and hoped that he would keep the overhead charges as low as possible.

The final version of this letter was dated 4th July 1951, and simply stated that Cobb would pay Vosper £10,000 for the design and construction of a craft to challenge the World's Unlimited Water Speed Record in 1952. If successful, Cobb would pay the actual cost in full, based on audited accounts, including normal commercial charges and profit. This assumed that the engine would be provided on loan, and Vosper undertook to do all reasonably possible to obtain further materials on a free issue basis, for which purpose Cobb would advise of any particular suppliers who might be appropriate. The agreed sum covered the design and construction of the boat and cradle, but no costs associated with transport, trials or insurance. Vosper had already expended a considerable amount on the project and suggested payment of half the £10,000 in the near future, with the balance when the boat was ready for trials. The letter ended expressing their determination to spare no efforts and their appreciation of the opportunity, as well as of Cobb's fine spirit in undertaking the venture.

On the next day, 5th July, Cobb replied confirming his agreement, and expressing the hope that the boat could be ready for trials in the early summer of 1952. However, both of them realised that there was yet much work to be undertaken, and that they were still awaiting the necessary confirmation from De Havillands. Meanwhile Cobb, who was going abroad on business, sent Vosper a cheque for £5,000 on the understanding that it would not be cashed until confirmation of the engine supply was received. This was forthcoming some three weeks later, when on 24th July, Halford reported that Boothman of the Ministry of Supply had confirmed in writing that one of their Ghost engines could be loaned for "a few months in the spring of 1952", provided that it was fully insured and did not require any serious modification for the purpose. Du Cane still refrained from cashing the cheque until the De Havilland Board ratified this agreement and agreed to play their part. Confirmation of this only came at the end of August, and was subject to any expenses being reimbursed. Technical advice, however, was to be provided free of charge.

Despite this delay in achieving formal confirmation of its availability, detailed technical discussion of the engine had already begun on 4th July when R D J Hawkes, De Havilland's Chief Installation Engineer, visited Vosper for the first time. It soon transpired that a standard Ghost Mk3 with bifurcated air intakes would be most suitable, but at around 230 m.p.h. the thrust, now estimated at some 4,500lb, would probably be insufficient. Hawkes suggested that a slight reduction in nozzle diameter would suffice to raise this to about 4,750lb; the figure Du Cane considered necessary. In view of the short duration of the required run, Hawkes did not think that the resulting increase in turbine blade temperature would be a problem. Alternatively, injecting water gathered by a small scoop below the hull would give some 10% increase in thrust. Probably this was rejected on account of the increased drag.

The actual installation in the hull appeared to offer few problems as very little modification to the standard engine was required, other than removing a number of engine driven accessories which would not be necessary.

Each run was envisaged as comprising a mile of "taxiing", followed by two miles acceleration, one mile over the course, and a further three miles to slow down, turn and taxi in preparation for a similar return run; a total of seven miles each way. A preliminary estimate of the fuel required for all this was around 50 gallons, which was evidently some relief to Vospers: They had allowed for an 85 gallon tank but it now transpired that the engine itself would be some 100lb heavier than they had previously been informed. Already the all-important weight target was being threatened. The size of the tank was not changed but at least it might not be necessary to fill it, saving some 250lb.

Ventilation of a wooden boat containing a very hot jet engine was also a problem, and Hawkes suggested arranging for a flow of air between the jet pipe lagging and the hull, the inside of the latter also being covered with a lightweight sheet of polished aluminium to reflect the heat. The positioning of the engine air intakes in order to provide satisfactory flow, whilst avoiding spray as far as possible was also discussed, although some ingestion of fresh water could be tolerated.

Hawkes proposed a full set of engine instruments as would be fitted to a prototype aircraft, and promised to send details. It was later arranged for these instruments to be provided on loan. Finally he suggested that Vospers might find it useful to look at the structural design of the Vampire or Venom aircraft cockpits, since these were also built of wood and had a similar layout where the pilot had to be fitted between the air intake ducts. For this purpose, he arranged for a visit to the Airspeed division of De Havilland, situated only a couple of miles away at Portsmouth Aerodrome. Taken over by De Havilland in 1940, Airspeed was the aircraft company founded in 1931 by Nevil Norway, better known perhaps as Nevil Shute, the author.

Vospers had already wasted no time in getting down to some detail in the structural design. It had always been clear that some care would be necessary with the cantilever arms supporting the rear sponsons. Not only would these be required to carry significant shock loads, but they would have to be attached to the hull in way of the engine and could not therefore continue very far inside the surface.

Such structural problems were an area where Railton was at home. He had returned to America at the end of June, but promised to give the matter some thought as soon as possible. To help him in this, Du Cane had sent him the latest copy of the construction plan which arrived in Liverpool just in time to catch his ship before it sailed. Railton must have spent part of the voyage across the Atlantic working on the problem because on 2nd July he posted a letter from Detroit enclosing freehand pencil sketches of an ingenious solution using steel components. This allowed the sponsons and arms to be easily detached for transport by undoing only four bolts, whilst presenting a very strong structure when assembled without impeding access to the engine bay. However, as he pointed out, there would be insufficient room for it in way of the main body of the engine, and the complete arms were rather heavy, at (he estimated) around 300lb. He suggested that a similar solution could be constructed using an aluminium alloy, but would have to be designed by a competent aircraft engineer.

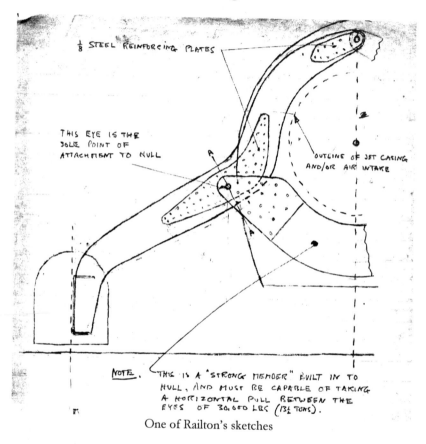

One of Railton's sketches

His sketches were passed to the Vosper Drawing Office, who appreciated their advantages but soon came across a number of problems: Firstly, the position of the forward cantilever was indeed in way of the maximum engine diameter, which would necessitate moving the arm forwards. This in turn would mean resiting the cockpit and fuel tank, and might also cause interference with the air intake ducts. There were several other structural problems and they also considered that the resultant weight would be nearer 450lb.

Probably these problems had been anticipated and discussed with Railton before he left the UK, because Du Cane had already approached the Chief Designer of Vickers Armstrongs, Joseph Smith, for advice. It was Smith who had taken over responsibility for the design of the Supermarine *Spitfire* when Reginald Mitchell died of cancer in June 1937, and took it successfully through many stages of development. His *Attacker* jet fighter, and its successor, the *Swift*, had very similar structural problems where the tailplane joined the rear fuselage in way of the jet pipe. Smith's team showed him how they tackled this and referred him to a number of sources of supply for the highly stressed aluminium alloys which they used.

Sir John Rix   *Vosper*

Meanwhile, John Rix had obtained the necessary licence from the Admiralty to build a "High Speed Experimental Craft". This General Licence No.SR/452 permitted Vosper to build vessels of any type under 100 gross tons, up to September 30th 1951. He replied thanking the authorities and pointing out that because of the necessary design work it would not be possible to build the craft by then. "However," he added, "we are accepting the fact that we shall be given permission even though this may commence after September 30th." This sounds like a skilful attempt at avoiding a further lengthy round of bureaucracy which might have been required to extend the date! At the same time, Rix sent a memo to the Drawing Office urging them to assess the amounts of material required as soon as possible so that he could apply for the licences which were also required for that, as he anticipated that because of the rearmament programme such things would soon become even more difficult.

Geoff Brading, the Chief Draughtsman, estimated that 12 cu.ft. of hardwood, 10 cu.ft. of softwood and 1895 sq.ft. of ply would be required. He had ordered most of the plywood, some of it faced with 18 gauge aluminium sheet, from the Aeronautical & Panel Plywood Co. by 9th August, but the amount quoted was still subject to some final tests of certain structural members, for which purpose he had asked for samples of the alloy faced ply. The dimensions of the latter composite indicate that it was probably intended for the planing surfaces, which were later to be changed to all aluminium construction. The Plywood Co. also sent him a sample of end grain balsa faced with aluminium, likewise for the purpose of riveting and bolting tests.

Final decisions also depended on the outcome of the ongoing model tests, which by now were concentrating on the possibility of incorporating some "vee" in the shape of the planing surfaces, and attempting to get some idea of the probable shock loadings on the boat. Such considerations obviously influenced the design of the structure, and therefore the choice and ordering of materials. These were subject to delivery delays, and in addition to the pressure on account of the construction licence, the loan of the engine had been agreed only "for a few months" the following spring. Although Cobb was reasonably sure that once they had their hands on it, the engine would not quickly be taken away, time was limited, and Du Cane had to finalise the configuration of the planing surfaces at the beginning of October.

One of the potential suppliers of light alloys suggested by Vickers Armstrong for the cantilever arms was Northern Aluminium, who had supplied some material for Cobb's land speed record car, and expressed keenness to assist again. However, before they had had time to discuss this in any detail, British Aluminium – a rival – had intervened in the shape of Dr. Ewan Corlett who was also very willing to advise on its use in the structure. Corlett is today remembered as the naval architect who was the prime mover in the salvage of Brunel's *Great Britain*, the technical adviser in her restoration, and author of her definitive history. In 1951 he had just completed a doctorate in the use of aluminium in compound structures.

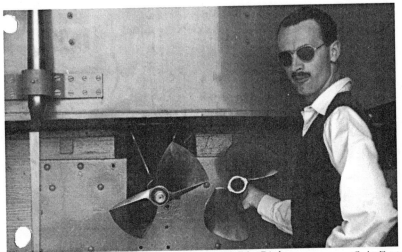

Dr. E C B Corlett with *Blue Bird*.   *Corlett Estate*

He was already involved with Donald Campbell's project to modify the Vosper built *Blue Bird* to proprider form, but considered that this would not result in any conflict of interests: He explained that commenting on "structural connections" was part of their normal service, although in the event he went further than that description might imply. He proposed a detailed design for the cantilevers which would permit them to be constructed without the necessity of complex heat or chemical treatment and using materials which British Aluminium would be able to supply in the required timescale. The necessary aluminium could not be supplied "off the shelf" but Corlett anticipated a "very quick" delivery of two months, which was in line with Vospers request that it be available by the end of November. "I don't know how this has come about" he wrote, "as normally our Works merely sneer when deliveries of this sort are asked for." He guessed that, luckily, other work requiring the same dies was scheduled then.

At a rather late stage - probably at a meeting on 23rd October - he also persuaded Du Cane to change the material used for the planing surfaces from wood to aluminium. This change, which was also influenced by the difficulty in obtaining the fastenings required for the equivalent wood structure, also led to the use of the same material for the forward planing surface. Du Cane's original intention of using alloy faced birch plywood in this area was soundly based on his considerable experience with previous Vosper boats, and this latter change was to be one which he always regretted. Both wood and aluminium are excellent structural materials; but mixing them may cause problems. Whether it did so in this case is debateable, and will be discussed later.

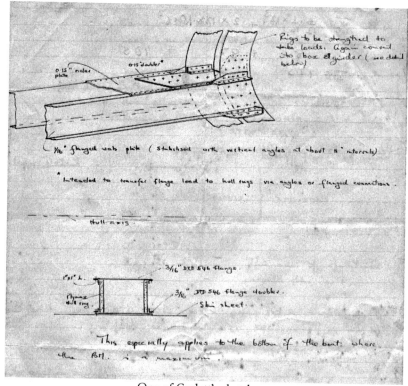

One of Corlett's sketches.

All eyes were concentrated on the most acute structural problem; that of the cantilever and ring bulkhead design. Du Cane was anxious to leave as little as possible to chance in the stressing of these vital parts of the structure, and at Corlett's suggestion he again asked for – and received – advice from both Vickers Armstrongs and Saunders Roe, the former in examining the stresses in the cantilever arms, and the latter in assessing the probable forces imposed by "punch" loads caused by the sponsons hitting waves. As has already been discussed, this was very much a matter of guesswork, but it seemed likely that those with experience of designing a jet propelled flying boat were likely to make the best guess! The file contains several diagrams which illustrate the assumptions made by them. Vickers Armstrong also replied with suggestions for some small modifications to the design of the cantilevers.

Du Cane and Cobb were trying hard to persuade all suppliers to offer favourable prices or even free issue of materials, and although Corlett was sure that British Aluminium would be sympathetic, he himself was not in a position to negotiate this. However, he pointed out that any offers might depend upon their dealings with Donald Campbell, as it would not be fair to offer different terms. Cobb himself negotiated with British Aluminium about this, and the metal was eventually supplied free of charge although this was not agreed until the spring of 1952.

Corlett also claims to have been involved in the choice of a name for the boat. Whilst lunching with Cobb one day, this topic came up. After a discussing a number of uninspiring options, Cobb remarked that his aim was to put the record out of reach of the Americans. "You could say", he commented, "that I am running a sort of crusade". "Yes" replied Corlett, "and you have just named the boat!"

Cobb liked the name *Crusader*, because, he said, a Crusader was a man who got out of his office and had fun! However, in mid October he had consulted his sponsors, Wakefield, who were very much against this name, and so in a letter he asked Du Cane to refer to it "by some job number, such as JC1 or something" for the time being, while he gave the matter further thought. Like all Vosper projects, it had already been given a sequential build number, 2456, which continued to be used by everybody for some time.

In the same letter he remarked that he had heard from Railton who obviously wished he could be present. Cobb had not encouraged him, as, he said, he could not afford to pay his expenses, but thought that Railton might find an excuse to come before long, especially if Du Cane would like to talk to him, and this might save some arguments later on!

Cobb was right: In November 1951 Railton paid another brief visit to the UK and spent some time discussing the structure with Corlett and Du Cane who were still not satisfied with the details. A further practical complication was the need to limit the beam of the boat during transportation by road to around 11 feet, and Corlett recommended making the sponsons detachable from the cantilevers at a point corresponding to this maximum width, in order to minimise the bending loads at the joint.

Several pages of pencilled calculations in both Railton's and Du Cane's handwriting have survived, relating to estimates of the loads imposed on the structure by wave impacts throwing the boat into the air. It is clear however that, of necessity, many of their assumptions about shock loads involved a considerable element of guesswork. One of Railton's early estimates assumed that a wave would be totally unyielding, resulting in a very high acceleration. Du Cane protested that although water was incompressible, "spill out" on either side of the sponsons would cushion the shock; in other words, the shape of the wave would be changed by the impact! "I am not for a moment trying to dispute your mathematics" he wrote, "but there is something wrong with a result of 220g!..... can you honestly believe that this boat would not be able to pass over a 3 inch wave?". After further calculations by both men, Railton modified his estimate to 11g, saying that to be safe it should be assumed that virtually all of the shock might be borne by a single cantilever at a time. This resulted in a design load of about 33,000lb. which Corlett considered was achievable without undue weight increase and sent a freehand sketch of the suggested arrangement.

Most of this discussion, aided by the advice from Vickers Armstrongs and Saunders Roe, concentrated on the design of the cantilever arms and their surrounding structure, rather than on the forward shoe and the actual planing surfaces, although similar calculations were carried out for these. In the pencilled notes, consideration of the known forces due to weight of the boat and thrust of the engine highlighted the fact that the forward shoe would normally be loaded much more than the sponsons, not only due to being nearer the centre of gravity, but also because of the bow down force caused by the jet thrust.

Although referred to generally as "aluminium" in the foregoing description, the material available from British Aluminium comprised a wide range of different alloys each having different properties, which also depend upon whether they are, for example, to be bent, welded, or extruded, and which can be modified by heat or chemical treatment. It must also be remembered that choice was limited by availability and the structural design could be affected by all these factors as well as the changing estimates of the imposed loads. During the design and construction of components made from these materials, Vosper made several test pieces to prove both riveting and welding techniques and these were tried in the British Aluminium laboratory. Corlett made many structural calculations, including some aimed at achieving the same panel stiffness as an equivalent wooden panel, which was of course relevant to the structure of the planing surfaces. Work on the actual planing surfaces was held up by Du Cane pending some of the laboratory test results. Probably these were carried out with a view to also employing similar structural techniques in other future boats, because the results of one particular test showed that "although perfectly satisfactory for normal shipbuilding use", welding had inevitably resulted in local softening of the metal, and Corlett thought it unsuitable for the sponson bottoms, where the absolute maximum strength was required.. This caused a further delay whilst an alternative alloy was supplied, and it is evident that several other late changes to the aluminium structure were made, right up until early April 1952.

The freehand notes by Railton and Du Cane also include calculations relating to the steering forces to be expected on the forward rudder. Although these were slightly more straightforward there were still many unknowns: The principle had been tested successfully on the model but it had only been possible to try small angles. It was obviously important to get the size of the rudder right; too small and it would be ineffective, too large and both drag forces and control forces would be unacceptable. At speed, little or no deflection would be necessary, but between runs the boat would have to turn 180 degrees, within the available space. For this reason, two rudders were made and the smaller one was fitted during initial trials.

A fixed stabilising fin was also to be attached to the rear of each sponson, similar to (although relatively smaller than) those fitted on the free-running model. The potential forces at speed on these and the rudder would be enormous, and so they were to be made from steel forgings. This led to a disproportionately large amount of correspondence with steel manufacturers Firth-Vickers and Thos. Firth & John Brown Ltd. who were asked to quote for materials and fabrication work. Delay was caused by design changes, letters crossing in the post, confusion over the suitability of various materials, and the inability of these companies to undertake fabrication. Finally, the imposition of a new control order coming into force on February 4th, 1952, made it illegal to deliver steel without proper authorisation from a Government Department. Somehow, all these obstacles were eventually overcome, the machining being carried out by Thompson & Taylor, but they were perhaps typical of the many problems which combined to delay the eventual delivery of the boat.

In order to control the rudder, approaches were made to various companies, some of whom had been involved in producing parts for the steering gear of Cobb's Railton Mobil Special land speed record car. Hydraulic operation was discussed, including the possibility of a device to limit the output torque to a safe value. Subsequent calculations showed that with simpler mechanical gearing, which could apply 60° of rudder movement with two turns of the steering wheel, the forces involved would make it impossible manually to apply enough helm to be dangerous. Just before Christmas 1951 Cobb persuaded the Adamant Engineering Company of Luton to provide the necessary gear free of charge. In March, 1952, they even agreed to supply a Bluemel steering wheel to his special requirements, with three spokes instead of the standard four. This could not be delivered until the end of May but the fact that by then this was acceptable, indicates that completion had already been delayed well beyond the spring.

Crusader is born.

The actual construction of the boat took place in a small shed near the wet dock at Portchester, and was under way by the new year of 1952. Except for the cantilever arms, the ring bulkheads supporting them, and the planing surfaces, the structure of the main hull and sponsons was mainly plywood. The principles employed were similar to those used on De Havilland Vampire and Venom jet fighters. The backbone, or keel, consisted of two girders fabricated from birch ply capped with spruce to which were fastened ply formers.

Longitudinal spruce connecting stringers formed the shape and the whole was covered with a double skin of 1/16" diagonal grain birch plywood running in opposite directions to achieve monocoque strength. At the bow, this necessitated a fairing, built on a jig, by Saro Laminated Wood Products, at Whippingham, Isle of Wight.

The Aeronautical & Panel Plywood Co., who had lately changed their name to William Mallinson & Sons, had agreed to supply the plywood at a discount and were anxious to make a press release. Du Cane commented to them that this material, considered purely on its tensile properties, could equal most heat treated aluminium alloys on a basis of strength-to-weight ratio, and when used in a panel had the advantage of greater thickness thereby lessening the likelihood of buckling. However, he asked them not to quote him as the source of this statement as he did not want to upset British Aluminium! Perhaps he was already slightly regretting being persuaded to use aluminium for the planing surfaces themselves.

Hawkes of De Havilland, on a visit at the end of the first week of January to discuss the fuel system, reported that there was little to see but a few frames. Robert Du Cane had tested some of the spruce and rock elm which had been delivered and, finding the moisture content a little high, had to arrange for it to be kiln dried to ensure that gluing would be satisfactory. This no doubt caused a slight delay.

Hawkes' visit was one of many during the build period and the associated notes contain many small details on the engine installation. For example, the fuel tank was to be pressurised by a pump, the pressure being regulated by a relief valve in the pipe.

The same system had been used on *Blue Bird*, and the original valve had been returned to De Havilland when the Goblin turbine was removed. Hawkes had brought the same valve back with him, and handed it over to Captain Basil Cronk, Vosper's Chief Engineer.

As well as advising on the installation of the engine, Hawkes was also able to suggest various fellow members of the aircraft industry who could supply sundry components, and could perhaps be persuaded to do so free of charge. He lunched with John Cobb early in the new year of 1952 and told him that he hoped to thus be able to source the air intakes and engine cowlings, complete with flush fasteners.

Cobb had also been negotiating with some of the companies who had supplied materials for his land speed record car, such as paint manufacturers Cellon. Graviners, who had supplied equipment for *Blue Bird* in its various forms, agreed to fit fire detectors to the boat itself and to loan fire extinguishers to be carried in attendant craft. GKN supplied some 2,000 stainless steel nuts and bolts, and also went to some trouble to source some such items, which were not in their own product range, from other makers.

Smiths Instruments, who had supplied the air speed indicator for *Blue Bird*, agreed to supply a similar instrument, as well as to provide all the various engine instruments on loan. The pitot head providing the dynamic pressure for this A.S.I. was mounted on a short mast fixed to the bow, and the final Fairey wind tunnel tests in April 1952 confirmed the suitability of this location.

On the 8th April Cobb wrote to Du Cane that he had finally decided to stick with the name *Crusader*. He later remarked to Railton that quite a few people seemed to like it, and nobody had come up with a better suggestion

There were continuing delays, due largely to the design and construction of the cantilever arms and ring bulkheads. All concerned were evidently most concerned about the problems of not only estimating safe design loads but of achieving the necessary structural strength with the available material and suitable manufacturing processes.

Building the hull   *Vosper*

The programme inexorably slipped back. On 21st March
Du Cane had written to Hawkes that Vosper should be ready for
the engine in mid May, but by 9th May this had changed to the
first week in June. Railton was due to visit in early June, when
Du Cane had to go to Brazil on other business. He left the
former a letter apologising for this and saying that they had had a

terrific job with the construction of the cantilevers and associated ring bulkheads, but hoped that this would be complete by his arrival, after which there would not be much left to do. However, the struggle was not quite over: in mid June John Rix issued a memo that the Shipyard were to have the hull ready for machinery installation by 1st July.

The air intake ducting appears to have been another problem. Hawkes had suggested that Folland Aircraft, conveniently located at nearby Hamble, might be persuaded to manufacture this, but after some delay, Follands passed the enquiry on to a subcontractor of theirs, Clip-On, at Swanwick, also nearby. Vosper provided suitable jigs, which were delivered to Clip-On in late May. Cobb and Du Cane visited their factory at the end of June to view progress, but it was not until mid July that the port duct was received, with the starboard one to follow a few days later. Clip-On had apparently agreed to supply these at cost, and provided an approximate figure for what was probably a tricky one-off job. Hawkes had originally hoped that these might be obtained free of charge.

A revised programme issued at Vosper on 25th June called for all hull work to be completed ready for the engine by 7th July, and for machinery and electrical installation to be complete by 21st, except for the intake ducting, which was to be complete by the end of the month when Cobb was due to inspect the mock-up of the cockpit layout. This only left final testing and painting.

Arrangements for launching and recovering *Crusader* were discussed as it was important during trials to be able to move her easily to and from a workshop ashore rather than try to carry out work afloat. Railton was very much against using a trolley and slipway and advocated use of a crane. Lifting the boat directly would be more convenient than handling it on its cradle but would necessitate suitable slinging points which, as one of them would be over the engine, was not straightforward. If attached directly at the engine trunnion there would be an undesirable horizontal component of the sling load, and further bracing of the hull would only add more weight. A separate "T" shaped slinging girder was designed in order to solve this problem.

At the end of May Cobb applied for a Certificate of Registration from the Marine Motoring Association, who issued the number K6, and charged the sum of seven shillings and sixpence (37½ p.).

Just before Christmas 1951 thoughts had begun to turn towards a suitable stretch of water for trials, and for the actual assault on the record. Bearing in mind the desirability of seven miles of clear water, neither Windermere nor Coniston seemed ideal and Du Cane wrote to a friend, Sir Ivar Colqhoun, for information about Loch Lomond. Sir Ivar's father had provided a base for Kaye Don when he had broken the record there twenty years previously. Sir Ivar replied to Du Cane with great enthusiasm, offering facilities and advice.

In February, 1952 Railton, who remembered rough water at Loch Lomond before the war when Malcolm Campbell had tried it with *Blue Bird* K3, wrote to Cobb that he thought it could be written off as impossible in August, presumably because of pleasure craft. He also knew that Donald Campbell had found the five miles at Coniston too short for comfort, and reckoned the boat did indeed need seven clear miles to be reasonably free from the anxiety of running out of water.

Cobb preferred Coniston but nevertheless he and Du Cane arranged a date to visit Loch Lomond. This was cancelled later, probably following a lunchtime discussion in early April over the charts of the Loch. Except at the northern end where it became rather narrow and remote from Sir Ivar's facilities near Luss, not even Loch Lomond could offer much more than three miles of suitable clear water.

In early April, Cobb spent an interesting day at the De Havilland factory at Hatfield, "playing about with the Ghost engine", he reported to Railton, and also was given a flight in the Ghost powered two seat Venom then in production for the RAF. Later that month he left for Madeira on holiday no doubt using the new flying-boat service, having arranged to visit Coniston and Windermere immediately on his return. Probably Du Cane's primary aim was for discreet initial trials whereas Cobb was already focusing on taking the record, currently standing at 160.32 m.p.h.. With luck, Coniston might suit both these objectives.

On 28th April 1952 they were flown up to investigate both lakes by Sir Raymond Quilter, of the GQ Parachute company, in his Dragon Rapide. He was something of a character, whose eyesight reputedly necessitated a magnifying glass to read some of the the cockpit instruments. It must have been an interesting trip! At Coniston they saw the sad remains of Donald Cambell's old Vosper built *Blue Bird*, which had been lying on the slipway since being written off the previous September when a propeller blade had failed at speed.

Sir Raymond Quilter   *Sir Anthony Quilter*

Two days later Cobb wrote to Railton that Coniston had been "like a sheet of glass" and that he was impressed by its straightness and width but that the facilities were nil and the cost of laying them on "would be a very serious matter." He did not like Windermere because he felt the greater width would mean one would be inclined to "get lost" at high speeds, and in identical weather conditions the surface had a slight ripple. On the other hand, the facilities there were superb. He was therefore in a quandary and asked for Railton's views.

Railton replied firmly favouring Windermere, saying in the initial stages there was bound to be a lot of messing about and the state of the water would be less important than facilities for working on the boat. He repeated that both lakes would be uncomfortably short and to reach anything like 200 m.p.h. would necessitate eventually going elsewhere. Du Cane certainly agreed with this.

This was where the GQ Parachute Company could help, and Quilter was full of ideas relating not only to braking parachutes for the boat, but also for safety devices for its occupant. Du Cane had first approached him in connection with a suitable life jacket for Cobb, pointing out that, in the event of the pilot being thrown out, automatic inflation was essential because an already inflated jacket would be cumbersome to wear and would in any case be stripped off when the wearer hit the water at speed. It was also most likely that he would be unconscious and therefore unable to operate any mechanism.

Quilter responded enthusiastically saying that he had just obtained a dummy for use in developing such devices, which was "true to a man in all characteristics" and he suggested doing trials on life jackets by dropping the dummy from a low flying aircraft, or projecting it with a rocket! He had also thought of providing the pilot with a personal braking parachute which would operate automatically to control his entry to the water. He commented that for this to work, the unfortunate victim would have to be thrown high in the air and clear of the boat, but he had considerable data from ejection seat trials. This particular scheme does not seem to have been pursued further, but it is interesting to speculate whether it, or any of Quilter's other ingenious ideas, could have saved Cobb. A suitable automatic "Mae West" life jacket was loaned by the Frankenstein company, who also made him a "Yachtsman's suit" of oilskins.

With the problem of limited length of clear water in mind, Quilter spent some time developing a suitable braking parachute for the boat, which was stowed in the headrest behind the cockpit and would have been ejected by a mortar. When deployed, this drogue would have caused a sudden deceleration which Quilter at first suggested might be as high as 2 or 3g. After further work the initial drag was set at 2,500lb, which, although only about 0.5g would have been enough to throw the pilot out, so he recommended that Cobb wore a GQ "Z" Type harness which would stand over 25g. He considered that such a harness should be worn anyway; for example, in the event of capsize, the structure of the boat would probably protect him, and an automatic device could release the buckle following immersion.

Du Cane also sought advice on harnesses from Geoffrey Tyson, the Saunders Roe test pilot responsible for the trials of the

A1 Flying Boat fighter. Tyson gave the matter careful thought and concluded that on balance, it was better to wear such a harness.

Saro A1 fighter prototype   *Solent Sky*

Firstly, he considered that in the case of an accident without a harness the pilot would suffer serious injury from surrounding structure when thrown out of the cockpit. Secondly, having done high speed rough water runs in the A1 both with and without harness, he did not believe the pilot could feel secure and be able to handle the craft accurately unless tightly strapped in. Such considerations in his view outweighed any anxiety about the possibility of being trapped under the inverted craft and drowned. If the pilot worried about that, he wrote, he shouldn't be there anyway.

Cobb however, although he had considerable experience flying as a ferry pilot during the war, was of the old school where cars or boats were concerned, saying that in his racing cars (which gave a pretty rough ride around the track at Brooklands) he was able to brace himself adequately in the cockpit with his left leg whilst operating the accelerator pedal with his right. He had requested that the boat be fitted with both hand and foot throttle controls which would be rigidly interconnected, presumably because this arrangement might further reduce any difficulty of operation under rough conditions. However, he was willing to give the harness a fair trial at some point. Probably, like Tyson, he was not one to worry excessively about accidents and thus discounted any advantages which the harness offered in what he considered to be hypothetical disaster situations.

Railton, Cobb and Du Cane at the press conference.   *Hulton/Getty Images*

Although all concerned preferred to avoid publicity as much as possible, particularly before anything had been achieved, Cobb realistically pointed out that it was beyond their control to stop any references in the press, especially as an ever increasing number of people would now be getting to know what was going on. So Angus Barr was appointed Press Officer by Wakefields, and on 1st July 1952 at the Royal Automobile Club, Pall Mall Cobb gave a press conference at which details of the boat were explained as well as being handed out in writing.* The wording of this had been carefully agreed between Railton, Cobb and Du Cane, explaining that *Crusader's* rather revolutionary layout had originally been suggested by Railton, and the subsequent design and construction had been carried out by Vosper in co-operation with British Aluminium and the De Havilland Engine Companies (Some of the others who had helped asked not to be mentioned). Despite this, the press immediately announced that Railton was the designer, which caused embarrassment and dismay all round.

* see appendix 1

At this press conference, Cobb also announced that he would carry out the first trials at Windermere. With the insurance of the braking parachute it might well have been safe to exceed 160 m.p.h., but by then all concerned must have agreed that sooner or later a larger area of water was going to be necessary. Railton had already suggested Loch Ness, saying that from merely looking at the map it looked an obvious choice. He observed that perhaps the Monster would prove a nuisance, or there might be too much traffic passing through the Caledonian Canal. A potential base had been identified at Temple Pier, near Drumnadrochit, and after Wakefields had made a preliminary approach to the owner, Alec Menzies, and the local authorities, Railton and Cobb had visited the Loch, probably some time in June. With them went George Eyston, a director of Wakefields, and another ex holder of the Land Speed Record, friend and rival of Cobb, who was now to be Cobb's Team Manager for the attempt on the record.

George Eyston   *Castrol*

On July 7th the American, Stanley Sayers, changed their plans by raising his record to 178 m.p.h.. Cobb wrote to Du Cane that he was neither surprised nor dismayed at this, but commented that it was a good thing that this had not happened just after he had done something slightly slower. Clearly, an extra 20 m.p.h. was considered too much for Windermere, so, on 21^{st,} a further announcement changed the location to Loch Ness, stating that a greater length of water would be required. A rough calculation supports this, showing that to stop within one mile from 200 m.p.h. with an adequate safety margin might have been marginal, even with the braking parachute. Years later, Donald Campbell's next *Blue Bird* was equipped with a water brake.

Towards the end of July completion of *Crusader* was almost in sight. The final covering of doped fabric on the hull had to await the fitting of the air ducts, and following the trial installation, the engine had to be temporarily removed to permit completion of piping, electrics and the surrounding heat deflector plating. The boat was weighed on 21st and the completed all-up figure calculated at 6241lb. The pilot's seat was being specially made by Rumbolds in London, who promised to have it ready for collection by Friday 25th July, and the engine was due to be replaced by Saturday 26th. Cobb was scheduled to inspect a mock-up of the cockpit the following Wednesday 30th, so that weekend and the following week must have been very busy. As a result of the inspection, Cobb asked for a modification to the throttle arrangements, and a single lever control unit was quickly supplied by Bloctube Ltd. of Aylesbury, free of charge.

Roll out   *Vosper*

The shipyard was due to shut down during the first two weeks of August for annual holidays, but Du Cane and some of his workforce carried on working. Nevertheless, it was not until Friday 8th that *Crusader* was rolled out of her shed and anchored with steel cables for an engine run-up ashore, at which Hawkes was present to supervise.

A memo in Du Cane's handwriting (Jean Carpenter having gone on holiday) reads *"Crusader ready for run up ashore 10.30 a.m. - after sat(isfactory) trials possibly put in water. Boats reqd. Janet, Snipe, Jolly Boat."*

Wakefields had decided to make a 16mm film and the opening shots show the boat, only half painted, being worked on in the open. Probably that same day she was then hoisted into the Portchester wet dock and Du Cane climbed aboard, also being captured on film. Railton too appears, among the spectators, but there is no sign of Cobb.

Completion

Castrol/Vosper

In view of the fact that the trials would now take place nearly 600 miles away, it was highly desirable to carry out at least some basic testing whilst still within reach of the shipyard. On 11th July Du Cane had written to the Harbour Master at Poole, where some slow speed trials of the jet version of *Blue Bird* had taken place, asking whether something similar could be permitted. He still hoped to do this if there was time after the boat was completed, but meanwhile seized this opportunity for a quick sea trial next to the Portchester Yard, although obviously there would be severe limitations due to space. On that day, the water turned out to be quite rough, but he pressed ahead, driving the boat himself, and was enveloped in spray. Speed was very limited and it was evident that some difficulty would be experienced in getting over the "hump". In the transition stage, the sponsons threw up a great deal of spray. The trial, also recorded on the Wakefield film, was abandoned, probably for fear of the engine ingesting too much salt water, although Du Cane commented to Hawkes that, despite what others may have thought, she should have been a perfectly good proposition in those conditions up to 70 or 80 m.p.h.

The Mae West life jacket which he is seen wearing in the film was probably the one loaned to Cobb by Frankensteins, because the previous week he had written to them, asking for a further supply of salt tablets and gas cylinders used in the mechanism, saying that he had accidentally triggered the inflation.

Portchester Yard   *Vosper*

Work continued during the second week of Vosper's shut down, and by the end of the holiday final painting and finishing was complete. The boat was put back in the wet dock, probably because Du Cane was still hoping for another trial run at Portchester, if not at Poole. On Tuesday 19th he replied in answer to an enquiry from a local newspaper that he was still not sure whether this would take place. However, time had run out as Cobb was anxious to get up to Loch Ness before the end of summer. There were no further trials and by Friday 22nd *Crusader* was on her way to Scotland, pausing at the New Malden Depot of Adams Brothers, who were responsible for transporting her and who agreed to allow her to be displayed to the press there en route.

New Malden

After that the next stop was Drumnadrochit, where she arrived on Tuesday, 26th August, 1952.

Loch Ness.

Loch Ness forms a major part of the Great Glen, the geological fault which runs from south west to north east for over one hundred miles, dividing Scotland in two. Nature has not quite filled all of the Glen with water, but this omission has been corrected by the Victorian engineer Thomas Telford to create the Caledonian Canal, allowing shipping to pass direct from the Irish Sea to the North Sea, via a number of locks. Loch Ness itself is almost dead straight, twenty six miles long, and between one and one and a half miles wide, stretching from Fort Augustus at the south western end, almost to Inverness, where the canal opens on to the Moray Firth. The road between the two towns runs along a narrow ledge, close alongside the north western shore, about fifty to a hundred feet above the water for virtually the whole length. The mountainous sides of the loch plunge straight into the water and continue on down without a break, resulting in a great depth close to the steep rocky sides. About two thirds of the way to Inverness, the almost straight shoreline is broken by a saw tooth shaped bay, around which the road makes a detour, passing through the village of Drumnadrochit, where it is joined by the road from Glen Affric, which lies some twelve miles to the west.

The potential base which had been identified, and which Cobb, Railton and Eyston had visited earlier in the summer was at Temple Pier. This was conveniently located near the northern end of this bay, about half a mile from the centre of the village, and overlooked by the main road, some fourteen miles from Inverness. A mile away across the water, on the opposite side of the bay, stand the ruins of Urquhart Castle, a picturesque landmark on a headland commanding an excellent view of much of the loch. The team had decided that Temple Pier would be ideal, and the owner, Alec Menzies, who thought it would be a wonderful venture to bring to the locality, had agreed enthusiastically to their request. They arranged for some repairs to be made to the old pier, and to the large shed nearby, which was fitted with high doors, clad in polished aluminium for lightness. Electricity and a telephone were also installed. A second shed was soon filled with barrels of fuel and oil, starter batteries, and all sorts of spares.

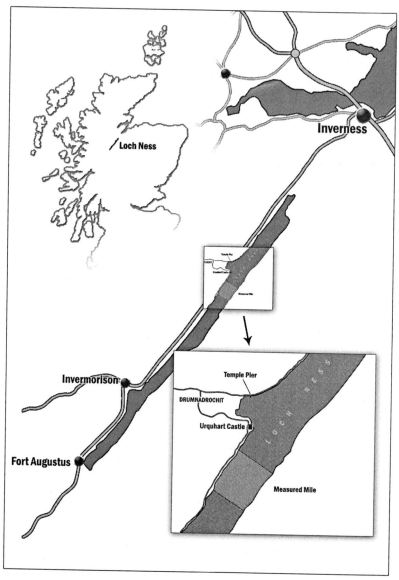

Architech

A caravan was placed on the site as team headquarters and a Ferguson tractor hired to move *Crusader* around on her trailer. This was to be driven by Bert Denley, who had been George Eyston's co-driver for many of his racing and record-breaking exploits.

Naturally the expected arrival of *Crusader* and the team aroused great interest in the area and it was anticipated that local hotels would be heavily booked by enthusiastic spectators. The Inverness Courier reported that even the Loch Ness Monster had put in an appearance not far away from Drumnadrochit a few days before the boat arrived.

Cobb and Railton arrived in Inverness over the weekend of the 23rd and 24th August and set up base in the Caledonian Hotel. On Monday, accompanied by George Eyston, they met J. G. McLellan, a local civil engineer who undertook to survey the measured mile. They then took a trip on the *Astrid*, a local fishing boat brought in to act as a mother ship for *Crusader*, to have a good look at the loch for themselves.

Astrid   *Highland Archive*

To handle the expected demands of the press, Angus Barr, Wakefield's Publicity Officer, announced that he would be resident at the Station Hotel, Inverness, from 25th August, and on the day that the boat arrived at Drumnadrochit – Tuesday 26th August – the press was already waiting. The weather was described by one reporter as rain-swept and mist-wreathed, a foretaste of what was to come.

To limit *Crusader* to a roadworthy width, and to spare the bearings of the engine from damage due to jolting during the long road journey, the sponsons and the Ghost had been removed and transported separately, the latter on suitable shock mounts. The first job therefore was to reassemble the boat and test the engine. The Vosper and De Havilland fitters got straight down to these tasks, whilst other members of the team surveyed the loch to decide where to erect the posts for the measured mile.

A Coles mobile crane had been brought in from Sunderland to enable *Crusader* to be launched into the loch, and this was first employed to lift the engine back into place. As the shed was not large enough, this activity took place in the open and a large crowd quickly gathered to watch from beside the road. The stone wall conveniently prevented unauthorised incursions to the site, whilst the height of the road above the shore afforded the spectators an excellent vantage point from which to view the activity around the red and silver monster.

Spectators at Temple Pier   *Hulton/Getty Images*

As well as reassembling the boat, there was equipment such as fire extinguishers and the Pye radio to install and test, and the press eagerly seized upon such snippets of information, gleaned from interviews with a shy and reluctant John Cobb, whilst awaiting some real action. The use of radio for communication between the pilot and the support craft was then something of an innovation in record breaking and some attention was also paid to the fact that the boat herself was the first to be specifically designed for jet propulsion.

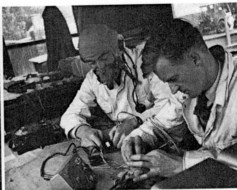

Checking engine and radio equipment   *Hulton/Getty Images*

Although shy of publicity, Cobb was keen to ensure a good relationship with the local population, and paid a courtesy visit on the Provost of Inverness, Jimmy Grigor, on Thursday 29th August. He was also conscious of local views on the keeping of the Sabbath, and decreed that no trials of *Crusader* would be carried out on Sundays. During his few weeks in the area he made a lasting impression on the inhabitants, particularly the children at the Glen Urquhart school. He never seemed to be too busy to show them over his boat or to sign their autograph albums.

The location chosen for the trials course was within easy reach of Temple Pier, extending beyond Urquhart Castle to the south, allowing for two miles acceleration or deceleration and turning each side of the measured mile itself. Posts were carefully set up to mark the latter, and it was suggested that because of the very high speeds now being reached in such ventures, that in future automatic electronic timing would be essential in order to achieve the necessary accuracy, although one reporter commented that in this case, fortunately, *Crusader* was expected to exceed the existing record by such a large margin that such accuracy would not be critical.

Despite optimistic predictions by the press of water trials beginning on Thursday, 28th August, it was only that evening that George Bristow and his De Havilland team were ready for their first engine run. The boat on her cradle was turned so that the jet exhaust pointed out over the loch, and the engine was started. For the first time, the sound echoed around the hills and could be heard several miles away; a characteristic moan which may well have been the reason for the Ghost being so named. At close range, of course, it was deafening and mechanics and spectators alike pressed fingers into their ears. Nowadays of course, Health and Safety Regulations would probably make the wearing of ear defenders mandatory for anybody within 100 yards!

Engine test

Hulton/Getty Images

Angus Barr issued a bulletin announcing that trials were now about to start and that running might take place, weather permitting, on any day except Sundays. A warning to other craft to keep clear followed, and the public were asked to refrain from boating on the loch during calm conditions.

The boat was indeed put in the water on Friday 29th August but apparently only to test it for leaks. Possibly conditions were deemed unsatisfactory for a first trial, as they were again on the following day, Saturday. Because Cobb had decreed that no trials would take place on Sundays, the press were left to find something else to write about until at least Monday. One report stated that some "rubber dinghies", used (it said) inside *Crusader's* hull to keep her afloat in the event of a leak, were mysteriously deflated, and so a guard was posted on the shed overnight. There is no mention of such a device in the files, but Peter Du Cane's son Charles remembers a sausage like buoyancy bag. Fifty years later, Gordon Menzies, son of the owner of Temple Pier, who was 12 years old at the time, happened to mention that although the shed was kept locked, he and his young friends knew of "a wee hole underneath", just large enough for them to squeeze through, to gaze with awe at *Crusader!* Any intruder would certainly have received rough justice from these guardians! Probably to save weight, the bag was removed; it does not seem to have been carried in the boat.

Launching at Temple Pier   *Corlett Estate*

As a further space filling story, Basil Cardew reported indignantly in the "Daily Express" that although the R.A.F. had enthusiastically offered to lend two boats and crews for tender and possible rescue duties, the Treasury had stepped in with a demand for payment for these services, which could not be met by the Team's limited budget. In the event this task was performed by *Astrid*, supported by several speedboats. These included a fast Windermere launch *Karuna*, which was to be sited at the far end of the course and fitted out as a refuelling vessel. It does not seem ever to have been needed for this as *Crusader*'s fuel tank proved large enough for a return run. Later, this fleet was joined by the 60 ton, twin screw motor yacht *Maureen Mhor*, which carried the Official Observer, timekeepers and Press.

On Monday, 1ˢᵗ September, bad weather again delayed the first trial, and Tuesday was no better except that the Duchess of Gloucester and her two sons came to visit and thereby saved the press from another blank day. John Cobb invited the two princes to sit in *Crusader's* cockpit.

Towing *Crusader* back past Urquhart Castle. *Corlett Estate*

It was not until the end of the first week that a final decision was made on the exact location of the measured mile. A narrow section was selected beyond Urquhart Castle where the banks fell at a very steep angle from the road on the north west side. The concrete posts had to be carefully lowered by ropes and George Eyston and his team braved very stormy weather to carry the necessary materials to the site by boat. On the south east side the positions were easily accessible from the road which runs nearer to the waters edge. In addition to the main posts on the NW shore, there was a smaller post for sighting and a "sentry box" shelter for the timekeepers.

At last, at dawn on Wednesday 3rd September, the surface of the loch was calm, but John Cobb, who had been briefly away from Inverness, was late arriving. George Eyston was most anxious not to miss the weather window, and so Peter Du Cane had a chance to drive the boat. All went well, and years afterwards he wrote *"I shall never forget the exhilaration of feeling the tremendous acceleration when, after a considerable bath from spray, she suddenly freed herself and gathered speed in a big way. This could, of course, have been expected, because…we had found the resistance/speed curve became a straight horizontal line after clearing the hump…"* This meant that under such conditions constant thrust would result in constant acceleration, so that to limit the speed it would be necessary to throttle back to achieve a delicate balance between thrust and drag. Du Cane also considered that the steering authority was rather limited, and recommended that Cobb considered trying the larger rudder which he had had prepared.

Crusader at speed

Leddy/Topfoto

After this run, Cobb arrived and took over for a further four or five runs, easily achieving over 100 m.p.h. The press commented ecstatically on her grace and speed, but on lifting the boat ashore the bow swung downwards and she was found to have shipped a significant amount of water. This seemed to be entering the hull during the transition phase when huge volumes of spray were generated, probably entering via the cockpit and the gap between the jet tailpipe and the transom.

Rudder

Vosper

Probably because steering was possible if not adequate, and it was not yet clear what effect it might have on maximum speed, the larger rudder was not fitted at this stage.

It was already evident that the transition over the "hump" was not easy, and that the longer it took, the more water was shipped. Weight was critical, both during this phase and at high speed, and so, in order to lighten the boat as much possible, the drogue parachute system was not carried. With the benefit of hindsight, this omission may have been significant, although it must be remembered that it had originally been intended as a means of stopping quickly in the restricted space available on the English Lakes, and therefore was not necessary on the vast expanse of Loch Ness. The possible need for it in different circumstances had barely been considered, and the firing switch was located on the dashboard, behind the steering wheel, where it would have been awkward to reach in a hurry. Du Cane had favoured a proposal to fit a ring switch on the wheel itself, but this never happened, either because it was not practicable, or because when the decision to use Loch Ness was made the system was relegated to being an interesting experiment rather than an essential emergency facility.

Cockpit   *Vosper*

Perhaps because Quilter had originally advocated the use of the safety harness in order to prevent Cobb being thrown out of the cockpit when the drogue was deployed, it too was left out. Tyson's recommendation that it was desirable in other circumstances was evidently ignored, in view of Cobb's previous experience in cars and his preference for wedging himself into the cockpit with his left leg.

Quilter was understandably upset that his drogue system was not fitted at the start of the trials, as he had spent a lot of effort on the development. Cobb promised to test both it and the harness in due course but wanted to test the boat itself first. He, at least, did not see either item as an essential safety measure, but he did wear the automatic life jacket loaned by Frankensteins.

Delay and frustration.

Waiting for the weather; Cronk, Cobb and Eyston.   *Hulton / Getty Images*

On Thursday, 4th September the weather again deteriorated and Du Cane, who had moved from the Caledonian Hotel in Inverness to the Glen Moriston Hotel, which was quieter and slightly nearer to the scene of action, but on the opposite side of Drumnadrochit, commented to his wife during the drive from the hotel that he thought conditions would be too rough to run. Nevertheless, Cobb went out again and managed an estimated 150 m.p.h. in a five mile run up the loch and back. Again the boat behaved well, despite the rough conditions.

After this run, it was discovered that the forward planing surface had suffered slight distortion and some remedial work was necessary. At this stage, probably because the water had been so rough, this does not appear to have caused any great surprise or concern. Cobb described handling the boat under these conditions as "like driving a London bus with flat tyres over cobblestones." (He had actually driven a London bus during the General Strike in 1926.) Angus Barr announced to the press that trials so far had been most promising but that Vosper had asked for time to make a thorough inspection of the hull, which would necessitate removing the engine. There would therefore be no more runs until the following week at the earliest.

Crusader showing her underside. *Corlett Estate*

During this time Du Cane anticipated having to return to Portsmouth for a few days, and he summarised the situation so far in a letter to Cobb. Although he did not mention the damage directly, he concluded that the prevailing conditions on Thursday *"were for all normal purposes unsuitable for a boat of this class."* He had, he acknowledged, asked Cobb to give her a *'good touseling'*, and considered that the results showed that better conditions should be selected in the future. He was obviously conscious of the difficulty they had experienced during the design phase in deciding what level of accelerations should be catered for, saying that he thought that the planned accelerometer trials were important in order to compare the actual levels with the design criteria. He commented to Cobb that he thought it probable that so far, 4 to 5 g had not been exceeded, although it was impossible to be sure. At this stage he was probably not unduly concerned, because although the boat was expected to go much faster, he assumed this would be in calmer conditions.

The promised loan of an accelerometer from the Marine Aircraft Experimental Establishment (M.A.E.E.) at Felixstowe had not yet materialised, although a suitable location for it had been arranged in one of the sponsons. The Superintendent, A.G. Smith, was very interested and had tentatively arranged to bring it up in a flying boat via the R.A.F. facility at Invergordon, just north of Inverness, to arrive on the previous Friday, before *Crusader* started trials. Unfortunately, due to a combination of availability, weather and aircraft serviceability this never happened, and their only two instruments were then required elsewhere. One of them was at the S.B.A.C. air show at Farnborough where, on Saturday, 6th September, whilst *Crusader* was still awaiting fair weather, a DH110 prototype jet fighter disintegrated during a low level run over the crowd, killing De Havillands' Chief Test Pilot, John Derry, together with his navigator and some thirty spectators. Significantly, the cause was structural failure of the wing, probably attributable to the enormous difficulty at the time of predicting stresses precisely and designing a lightweight structure to withstand them.

M.A.E.E.'s interest in *Crusader* was not purely academic as planing at high speed on three points was very relevant to high speed water based aircraft, which were at that time still regarded as a fruitful line of development, at least for military applications. Smith agreed to try to bring an accelerometer to Invergordon on 8th September; presumably when one became available after the S.B.A.C. show was over. He and Du Cane agreed that it would only be possible to obtain an approximate measure of accelerations because records would inevitably include the effects of roll and elasticity, but with only one instrument, and practical limitations on location, this was the best compromise available. Smith was probably aware of the danger of Treasury intervention preventing the whole exercise on cost grounds because he carefully mentioned that the delivery flight would be part of their air training flight test programme and that he would be able to do some other work, presumably at Invergordon, at the same time.

In the meantime it was necessary to repair the damage to the forward planing shoe, and this presented two problems: It was difficult to reach from inside the boat, and repair facilities at

Temple Pier were very limited. Hugh Jones, a Vosper fitter who had accompanied the boat to Drumnadrochit, was just able to squeeze into the hull, and Dennis Cronk and Charles Du Cane, the twelve year old sons of Vosper's Chief Engineer and Peter Du Cane respectively took turns to provide the necessary extra pair of hands to help, being the only other small members of the team!

Fast run   *Dr. Willie 'Frank' Macdonald.*

The only method of strengthening the planing shoe which was possible in the circumstances was to shore it up with wooden stiffeners, anything else requiring proper workshop facilities which were not available.

Owing to these repairs, the intervening Sunday, and the weather, there was no more running until Wednesday 10th September. Large crowds had gathered to watch from about 5 a.m., when *Crusader* was towed out into the Loch, but the water was at first too choppy for a trial. Conditions had improved by 2 p.m. when the water conditions were described as the best yet. Cobb managed a run in each direction, and *Crusader* was estimated to have achieved well over 180 m.p.h., fast enough to break the record, although with no timekeepers present this could not be claimed officially. A similar speed was achieved around noon on Thursday 11th when in a flat calm she made her fourth sortie, but under such conditions *Crusader* had difficulty in getting up onto the plane. After one of the speedboats had created a wash in front, she succeeded in making one run, but after turning round experienced similar difficulties and after several attempts operations were abandoned for the day. It was announced that Du Cane, who had returned to Portsmouth for a few days, would be coming back to "supervise" modifications, and there would be no more running for the time being.

After *Crusader* had arrived back at Temple Pier, ripples like a "dark hump" were sighted out on the Loch and gave rise amongst spectators to further reports of the "Monster". In fact, reported the Inverness Courier, this was a delayed action wake from the boats. The significance of this apparently went unnoticed at the time.

In such calm conditions, the problem of getting over the "hump" was a common problem with flying boats and was caused by difficulty in breaking the suction between the main hull and the water surface. As a temporary measure, in addition to using a speedboat to create waves, ropes were wrapped around the hull, in efforts to break this suction, with some success. However, the transition period was awkward and much water was still being shipped, mainly due to the cantilever arms causing a great deal of spray.

Further similar damage to the forward shoe occurred, and it was necessary to straighten it out again and further adjust the wooden shoring. During Du Cane's brief visit south, necessitated by other unrelated business, he discussed this problem with Dr. Corlett by phone. On 11th September the latter wrote a letter to him, addressed to Scotland, on the subject, pointing out that because the modulus of elasticity of wood was very different to that of aluminium, it was an unsuitable material to provide reinforcement. Where the two materials in contact were subjected to a load and forced to deflect by the same amount, the aluminium would inevitably take much more load than the wood, because the latter would deflect more readily. Unfortunately, as has already been pointed out, there was no alternative solution which could be implemented at Loch Ness.

Although this brief visit back to Portsmouth was necessitated by other matters, Du Cane also found time to deal with a few *Crusader* items. Mallinsons were still very anxious to capitalise on the use of their plywood in *Crusader* and had drafted press releases which, after a phone conversation, Du Cane modified slightly and returned

One problem was the price now being asked by Clip On for manufacturing the air intake ducts. This had turned out to be nearly three times their estimate, and as a result, Vospers had questioned it. The ongoing discussions were evidently causing friction on both sides.

Hawkes of De Havilland wrote concerning proposed modifications to the cantilever arms aimed at reducing the ingestion of water during the transition phase. Experiments were already in hand to find a solution to this problem, and various modifications to the shape of the arms were being tested in the AEW Haslar towing tank. A solution was developed, but there was never to be an opportunity to try it out.

Finally, there was the problem of the press who still insisted on referring to Railton as the designer of *Crusader*, causing continued embarrassment. The reasons for this were probably the previous long and successful careers of Cobb's unique cars, which Railton certainly had designed; the press release of July 1st which credited him with originally suggesting the layout; and the unanimous desire of Cobb, Railton and Du Cane to say as little else as possible to the press until something definite had been achieved. Despite this, Du Cane felt obliged to write to Group Captain the Hon. Max Aitken at the Daily Express, saying:

My Dear Max,

In connection with the "Crusader" trials, I hope you will not mind my pointing out that your correspondent up there constantly refers to Railton as the designer of "Crusader". This despite John Cobb's hand-out dated 1st July...

"We are quite content to do our job in reasonable obscurity, ...

"It is, however, rather a different thing when other individuals are handed the credit for such work...

"The last thing that we or I want is a publicity puff at this stage, but at least I do think that incorrect statements which could be damaging should be avoided...

"To be fair R.R. himself does not claim to be the designer so this is not a dig at him.

He also wrote to the Daily Telegraph in a similar vein, and Henry Loebl, the Chairman of Vosper Limited was prompted to write to Cobb, saying:

"I have been watching the progress of your trials with interest and have admired the way you have settled down to the job. Judging by what I have read, it seems that, given reasonable luck, you have the record in your pocket.

"I must say that my Board as well as the employees at Vospers, have felt very strongly the wide publicity to the effect that Mr. Railton is the designer.

"Both you and I know the truth of this matter, and I do hope that you will see your way, after the record has been taken, to correct this impression publicly.

John Cobb about to set off from Temple Pier   *Corlett Estate*

"An explanation would come better from you than from us, but for the sake of Peter Du Cane's reputation as a designer and Vosper's reputation as builders of fast craft, we cannot allow such an incorrect statement to persist.

"I wish you all possible success and once again express my admiration of your efforts on behalf of British prestige.

Cobb agreed and, although he was very busy at the time, wrote back to Loebl on 21ˢᵗ September, saying;

"...With regard to your remarks regarding publicity, I can only say that in the first instance this was clearly put to the press when we had a conference with them at the R.A.C. last July and I have done my best and shall continue to do so to see that they report matters accurately. But I feel certain

that you must realise very well that the ordinary newspaper reporter pays very little attention to accuracy and such inaccuracies as you have mentioned are bound to crop up. There is a slight excuse for it of course, in-as-much-as, Mr. Railton and myself have been associated together for many years now but one thing I can assure you is that Mr. Railton always hastens to disclaim being the designer of the boat and is just as embarrassed by inaccurate reports as I am. You can rely on me to do everything to give Peter in particular and Vospers all credit for the designing in any statement which I may make.

Certainly none of these exchanges were intended to belittle Reid Railton or his very considerable contribution to the project, and it is fitting to leave the last word on this topic to the man himself: Earlier in the year, he had written an article for an American magazine, in which he said :

"I am not a boat designer, and could have gotten exactly nowhere in these ventures without the skilled cooperation of experts in the structural, hydrodynamic and aerodynamic fields. My only responsibility has been **what** *to build, and* **why**. *The more difficult problem of* **how** *to build it has been left in more competent hands than mine."*

Cobb, Railton, Cronk, Du Cane, Eyston, Halford, Bristow.   *Hulton / Getty Images*

Back at Drumnadrochit, a meeting took place on Friday 12th September to review the situation. Having just returned from Portsmouth, Du Cane had a chance to be updated on the problem with the forward planing shoe. It had become clear that each fast run was causing distortion to the aluminium panel due to the heavy loading, and perhaps to the relative flexibility of the wooden stiffening, which Corlett had pointed out. However, there are indications that this stiffening was fairly robust and the trouble may have been due to the difficulty of anchoring it securely to the rest of the structure.

The angle of the aft sponsons had been arranged to help force the bow down to prevent porpoising, and although this had the desired effect, it also caused higher shock loads on the forward shoe. After each sortie extra stiffening was provided inside, but Du Cane knew that this was at best a palliative. He was now certain that the best solution was to revert to the original design of a thick birch ply panel, which would have created a more effective structure for the same weight.

Du Cane examining the forward step   *Hulton/Getty Images*

He therefore offered to take the boat back to Vosper's Yard, at Vosper's expense, to put things right. In fact, he beseeched Cobb to do this, but he was alone. Corlett, who would undoubtedly have supported him and thus perhaps won the day, was unable to be present. All the other members of the team were anxious to beat the record by a small margin, and only then to use the winter to modify the boat before returning in 1953 to put the record well beyond reach of any rivals for some time to come.

After a further examination of the boat over the weekend, Du Cane wrote what was to be his last letter to John Cobb. In it he reviewed the situation, saying that it was now clear that provided *Crusader* could be got over the hump in calm conditions, speeds in excess of 200 m.p.h. could be achieved. However, the structure at the after end of the forward planing shoe was unsatisfactory. In his opinion the aluminium sheet should be replaced by a stronger panel: thicker aluminium, steel, or plywood faced with aluminium, as he had originally intended.

He also pointed out that there was evidence of the transom moving relative to the forward ring bulkhead, and proposed further stiffening. The correct course, he repeated, would be to return the boat to Vospers shipyard where these structural problems could be attended to properly. Whilst there it would also be desirable to do something about the unstick problem, on which studies were already in hand. This would, he envisaged, result in the boat being returned in no more than a month in a fit state to take the record during 1952.

Under the crane at Temple Pier   *Highland Archive*

There were however, other contrary pressures on John Cobb in addition to the views of the rest of the team. The press, and public, of course, were expecting, if not demanding, action, regardless of any technical difficulties or inconvenient weather. More importantly, Cobb had just been appointed Chairman of the Falkland Islands Company and his business associates, who had never been keen on the project, had urged him rest on his land speed laurels. It seemed very likely that once he left Loch Ness this pressure would increase and he would not be allowed to return. In different circumstances he would surely have needed little persuasion to adopt the more cautious and logical approach, but to effectively give up when their goal was so close was unthinkable, and he therefore pressed Du Cane to think again.

The latter was thus persuaded to agree reluctantly to further running, but stipulated that this should only take place in very calm conditions, and that the boat should not exceed 190 m.p.h., which was of course quite enough to secure the record. He wrote: *"Provided we are allowed to do some interim strengthening, and it proves possible to get over the hump with the aid of speedboats, making use of near perfect conditions, there is a reasonable possibility you could capture the record."*

There is a typed draft of this letter in the file: He was clearly most unhappy at being forced to go against his better judgement and, quite apart from any personal feelings, concerned enough on behalf of his Company to consider some sort of formal disclaimer. He had written *"I must point out, however, that if for any reason you fail at this stage or further damage is caused, I feel sure you will accept the responsibility and all that it involves."* However, to write this to his friend obviously seemed too much; it has been firmly crossed out and he has written instead *"I understand you will accept responsibility for this course."*

George Eyston and Basil Cronk.   *Hulton/Getty Images*

The final runs.

The dye was cast and the timekeepers were sent for on Monday, 15th September, the day on which Du Cane wrote his final letter to John Cobb. That same day, a bulletin by Angus Barr announced that from three days thence, all runs would be timed. The press announced variously that the record attempt would be made on the following Thursday, or Friday. The timekeepers, headed by Arthur Bray, representing the Marine Motoring Association, arrived on Thursday and an attempt was made on Friday, 19th September, when huge crowds were expected and special buses were laid on from Inverness. The weather was gusty which made steering difficult. Although *Crusader* recorded 185.576 m.p.h. on the first run, Cobb was unable to line up with enough room for adequate acceleration for the return run, which therefore was at only 160.714 m.p.h.. The average of 173.14 m.p.h. was tantalisingly close, but not enough to break the record. *Crusader* had made the run about ¾ mile from the north west shore, which Bray considered was rather too far away for accurate observations by the timekeepers, and so he asked Cobb to make future runs nearer to the shore.

John and Vicki Cobb. *Hulton/Getty Images*

On Saturday 20th, the weather was again too rough, and to avoid a repetition of the unsuccessful record attempt, the opportunity was taken at last to change to the larger rudder. At the same time, the three ventilation holes in each web behind the forward planing shoe were enlarged into a triangular aperture in an attempt to improve the ability to get onto the plane (see photo, page 120). Gordon Menzies still has one of the pieces of aluminium thus removed, adorned with the autographs of Hugh Jones, George Hatch and Geoff Brading, members of the Vosper support team.

For the whole of the following week the weather was relentlessly awful; equinoctial gales driving everybody to the limits of frustration.

At last, on Saturday 27th the weather moderated just enough to test the new rudder and at 0830 *Crusader* made two runs down her normal central course, which were timed at 132 and 99 m.p.h., but although the steering was satisfactory conditions were quite unsuitable for a record attempt. The bored and impatient press were also cheered by Queen Elizabeth, the Queen Mother, who, on her way back to Beaufort Castle after the Spean Bridge Commando Memorial Ceremony, paid the team a visit.

Despite this brief respite, everybody else was bored and impatient too and it must have seemed that the bad weather had set in for the winter. Railton, overdue to return home to America, decided there was nothing else he could do and arranged to catch a boat from Southampton on 30th. Perversely, on 28th September, the day he left Inverness, the weather was at last calm. But it was a Sunday and Cobb stuck to his policy of observing the Sabbath.

On Monday 29th September the calm weather seemed likely to hold and everybody was up early to begin preparations in earnest. The yacht *Maureen,* carrying Arthur Bray, the timekeepers, and as many press reporters as could get aboard, set off down the loch to her station about half way down the measured mile. Everyone was in position by 0630 waiting for the expected calm. At 0930 conditions were still unsuitable and Cobb stood the team down. They repaired to the Drumnadrochit Hotel for breakfast, and waited. *Maureen* was instructed to stay where she was; the large motor yacht would have taken too long to return to Drumnadrochit and those aboard were relatively comfortable anyway.

By 1115 the weather had greatly improved and the decision was taken to go as soon as possible and before conditions deteriorated again. Everyone hurried to their stations; some were even reported as having been left behind in the rush and the Inverness Courier recorded the following day that "*the loch never regained its calm after the support boats were deployed.*"

Alec Menzies, going to see what was happening at Temple Pier, bumped into John Cobb as the latter stepped out of the caravan which served as an office. "Where have they taken *Crusader*, Mr. Menzies?" he asked. She was nowhere in sight, but when the pair reached the end of the pier they saw that she and the tender *Astrid* had been hidden from view by the nearby headland. At that moment a messenger from the radio van appeared saying that everything was ready, and Cobb went back to the caravan to say goodbye to his wife and other members of the party who were about to drive round to the course.

In the cockpit   *Corlett Estate*

Cobb went out to *Crusader* in a launch, and at this point there were other boat movements required to get everyone else back to their stations. George Eyston headed for the far end of the course in the fast launch *Karuna*, and Harry Cole and Hugh Jones proceeded in the same direction in the Vosper Jolly Boat. According to one report, just as they were setting out, *Maureen* appeared round Urquhart point. Perhaps the members of the press had become sufficiently impatient to persuade the skipper to return. It is hard to understand why Arthur Bray, who had available radio communication with the shore, would have permitted this or even seen the need for it. Cobb reportedly told *Maureen* to get back on station, which she proceeded to do as quickly as possible. At 1154 everybody was in place and *Astrid* started *Crusaders* engine. Amongst others, Basil Cronk and William Rees, the Pye Radio engineer, saw Cobb off.

Du Cane was stationed on the road, about half way down the measured mile, and in touch by radio with the timekeepers. As far as he could see, the loch was perfect but he passed a message to Cobb saying that the conditions near the (further) South bank were better than the North, where he was. He and Arthur Bray agreed that conditions were suitable but allowed about ten minutes for the wash from the launches to settle down. A few minutes later *Crusader's* start was announced over the radio and she soon appeared from behind Urquhart Castle point. He was delighted to see that she was running beautifully, but then to his alarm noticed a series of three waves moving out from the North bank into her path, which as the timekeepers had requested, was much nearer this side than previously.

Running perfectly. *Whyte/Highland Archive*

There was nothing which anyone could do and *Crusader* hit them with a smack which was clearly audible to the onlookers by the roadside. The engine note was heard to slow momentarily before accelerating again, but the boat began to porpoise, the bow bouncing violently. Cobb apparently cut the engine again and the speed began to reduce, but just beyond the end of the measured mile the nose suddenly went right down into the water and the whole boat disappeared in a huge cloud of spray and steam as the water rushed into the jet engine. Deceleration was extremely sudden; Cobb was thrown out of the cockpit and, after several violent bounces, came to rest in the water some hundred and fifty yards further on.

The final plunge

The spray quickly cleared leaving nothing to be seen but many small pieces of floating wreckage, and a brief glimpse of the tail of one of the sponsons as it sank beneath the surface.

In the sudden hush following the abrupt ceasing of the jet whine, the Vosper Jolly Boat was the first to reach Cobb, who was floating in his lifejacket. Harry Cole and Hugh Jones helped to pull him aboard and owing to lack of space he was at first propped up in a sitting position. This gave some of the spectators the impression that he was all right, and although it was later clear that he had died immediately, the story persisted for some time that he was alive when pulled out of the water.

By this time *Maureen* had arrived on the scene and Arthur Bray descended into the boat. He examined Cobb, who was laid on top of the engine casing. Visible injuries were to his jaw and right leg, and Bray thought that he was probably dead, but instructed the launch to get to the pier as fast as possible, where he had radioed ahead for a doctor and ambulance. Once out of sight of *Maureen* with her crew of press photographers, he looked at the body more carefully, but could detect no heartbeat.

Back at Temple Pier, Alec Menzies had heard *Crusader*'s engine cut out, and thought she was preparing for the return run when one of the radio team ran over; shouting that there had been an accident and an ambulance was needed. There was already a doctor on the loch, but it took half an hour to get through to the ambulance service.

Before the launch carrying Bray with Cobb's body arrived at Temple Pier, they were met by another launch carrying the local doctor, Dr. Willie 'Frank' Macdonald, who confirmed that Cobb was dead. Bray then had the unhappy task of confirming this to Mrs. Cobb, who had been watching from the shore. She was being looked after by Basil Cronk's wife, who as a result, had been obliged to leave young Dennis Cronk to his own devices at what had been a most traumatic moment for him too.

Burning the wreckage. *Gordon Menzies*

Bray then gave instructions for the boats and other craft to pick up as much wreckage as possible. The engine was several hundred feet down at the bottom of the loch, having taken with it most of the stern half of *Crusader*, none of which could be recovered. The remaining flotsam mostly resulted from the disintegration of the plywood bow section, and, at Mrs. Cobb's request, was later burnt at Temple Pier to frustrate souvenir hunters.

Crusader had completed the mile at an average speed of 206.89 m.p.h., the fastest speed then recorded on water, and almost 30 m.p.h. more than the existing record. Because there was no return run, this could not count as a record.

Epilogue.

The accident had come as a deep shock to everybody concerned, but the modest and kindly Cobb had made a particularly deep impression on the local people and on Wednesday afternoon, 1st October, a Memorial Service, conducted at the Royal Infirmary's Tweedmouth Memorial Chapel by the Provost of Inverness Cathedral, was packed to the doors and when the hearse left Inverness, thousands of people lined the streets in the rain to pay their respects.

Railton, who had heard the news just as he was about to board a Transatlantic Liner at Southampton, had immediately returned. He joined the congregation together with Eyston and other members of the team, as well as a large number of local dignitaries, all of whom came to bid farewell. There were numerous wreaths bearing motifs such as "A Gallant Gentleman" and "To a Gallant Crusader".

Before leaving Inverness, Du Cane wrote a letter to the Inverness Courier expressing thanks to the people of the Highlands for the welcome and the hospitality which he and other members of Vosper had received. Despite the terrible tragedy, there was nothing wrong with Loch Ness, he wrote; tomorrow, given the organisation and the men, the torch could be handed on.

John Cobb's funeral took place on Friday, 3rd October at the Church at Esher, near London. The family favoured a private funeral, but a large number of mourners attended. On 31st October there was also a memorial service at St Michael's Cornhill, in the City of London.

On the day of the funeral, Colonel Malcolm, the President of the Glen Urquhart Community Association announced that a memorial cairn was to be built at Loch Ness., and this was unveiled next to the road, opposite the crash site on 29th September, 1953: the first anniversary of the disaster. Today this monument continues to be maintained by the local community, and the memory of John Cobb, who spent only thirty five days amongst them, burns brighter here than in any other place.

Speculation as to the cause of the accident and what might have occurred otherwise continued for months and even years after the event, and this account would be incomplete without some mention of this.

Du Cane fully expected that there would be an official enquiry, (In fact, there never was) and immediately drafted a written statement with this in mind. In this report, he limited himself to a brief summary of events leading up to the accident and statements of fact based on his own observation of it. He deliberately avoided drawing any conclusions as to the cause, probably because he had not had time to examine all the evidence, nor would it have been proper to anticipate the findings of an official enquiry. In further notes, written two months after the event, he speculated whether the initial throttle reduction after striking the first wave was a deliberate precautionary measure, or involuntary, caused by the impact being transmitted to the throttle, the last part of the travel of which was particularly sensitive. He favoured the former hypothesis, and in any event it seems fairly certain that the subsequent and final throttle reduction was deliberate as soon as Cobb had realised that he was in trouble, and was able to operate the control. This may have proved difficult, as he was by then being severely buffeted by the porpoising motion.

Du Cane estimated that the maximum speed of the boat, on hitting the first wave, would have been about 240 to 250m.p.h. He based this on assuming a deceleration of 6m.p.h. per second over the second half of the mile, resulting in a loss of about 50m.p.h. in 8 seconds, which would mean that the accident occurred at about 200m.p.h., and it is difficult to understand how he reconciled this with the official average of 206 over the whole mile.

A modern analysis of the cine film taken over the entire length of the mile from the south bank of the loch, using facilities which were not available to Du Cane, suggests that the speed had stabilised at about 210m.p.h. when she hit the first wave, and that this might have caused Cobb to involuntarily open the throttle, perhaps losing his grip on it. After a slight delay, he was able to close it again until the speed had reduced to its former value, when he re-opened it. At this point he realised that something was wrong, and shut it down all together. One must remember however that throttle control would not have been easy because it was very sensitive near the maximum opening, and because there was a significant delay in the Ghost's response to adjustments. Moreover, Cobb was by then being severely thrown about in the cockpit; accurate control movements would have been very difficult as would reading the airspeed indicator.

The "spiky" nature of the raw speed graph is entirely due to unavoidable errors in measuring successive positions and distances from a small and indistinct image and does not represent true movement of the boat. Even the smoothed plot probably over estimates the short term accelerations.

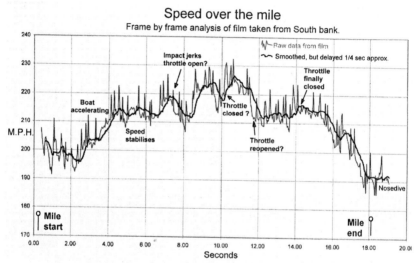

The maximum speed was almost certainly no more than 220 to 225m.p.h., although the deceleration once the throttle had been closed indeed averaged about 6m.p.h. per second. A useful cross check of this analysis is that the average speed over the mile agrees almost exactly with that actually recorded, but nevertheless it must be said that this suggested sequence of events is highly speculative.

It would have been most uncharacteristic of Cobb deliberately to ignore the advice not to exceed 190m.p.h., especially by a margin of 30 to 35m.p.h.. However, the fact that he did exceed it can perhaps be explained by the very flat drag curve and the consequent difficulty of checking the acceleration. It may also be that, mindful of the possibility that his business commitments might not allow him another attempt, he was privately anxious to exceed the magic figure of 200m.p.h..

One report, unconfirmed by anything in Du Cane's files, suggested that a stop was fitted to the throttle but removed by Cobb himself. Fitting seems unlikely as full power would be required to get over the hump, and anyway, to remove it would also have been most uncharacteristic of Cobb.

At a post mortem examination the day after the accident, it was confirmed that he had died instantaneously from shock, due to severe injuries. In fact, as Geoffrey Tyson, the Saunders-Roe test pilot, had only too correctly predicted, lack of a safety harness meant that he was thrown violently through the windscreen and was severely injured on the way. Had he been wearing the harness he would at least have been spared this, and might have been shielded from the worst of the impact with the water by the collapsing bow structure, before being automatically released from the harness. His automatic lifejacket functioned correctly, even though it too was lacerated, and it is thus perhaps just possible that he could have survived.

Whilst this is wild speculation, Du Cane, in notes which he wrote some two months after the event, commented that had the drogue parachute been available and had Cobb been able to deploy it as soon as the trouble started, it might have saved him. The resulting deceleration would have been much quicker, and the drag of the chute would also have helped to raise the bow and thus reduce the load on the forward step.

Some further mention of the structural problems of the forward step which evidently caused the disaster is appropriate, although it must be said that this too is somewhat speculative. The structural drawings show aluminium bottom stringers similar to those used in the sponsons. This is confirmed by a letter dated October 1952 to M.A.E.E. at Felixstowe, in which Du Cane mentions that Corlett recommended the 3/16" aluminium plate and the 1" x 1¼" x ⅛" aluminium stiffeners used. The change from a birch ply panel was in part due to difficulty in obtaining suitable fasteners. Du Cane also says that a load of 30,000lb was assumed at the aft end of the step, but that "we did not do any worthwhile calculations here as we did not know to what extent this force could be concentrated." This is probably the root of the problem, and it is significant that the forward shoe was intended to be more heavily loaded than the sponsons, which showed no signs of distress.

The forward planing surface was being pushed up between the bulkheads, suggesting that the wooden bulkheads themselves were adequate but the bottom, even with aluminium stringers, was not.

As Dr. Corlett had warned, the problem with using wood for temporarily reinforcement is that wood components designed to share the bending load with the aluminium would be unable to do so fully before deflecting well beyond the breaking point of the latter. The wooden reinforcing added at Loch Ness apparently comprised wood blocks forced down onto the bottom and retained by screws through the wooden sides of the forward shoe. This structure was probably "over designed" in the sense that the wood blocks themselves would have taken the necessary load without allowing excessive deflection of the aluminium, but unfortunately it proved impossible to fasten them securely to the sides of the shoe: the screws were forced upwards.

One can imagine that the initial wave impact locally forced the lower surface of the step, together with the wood blocks, upwards, except at the after edge where it was supported by the rear bulkhead, which in turn was reinforced by the rudder post. This resulted in a sort of inverted scoop, the excessive lift from which threw the bow clear of the water, whence it fell back with a further violent impact, and this process was repeated until the aluminium surface was eventually ruptured. There was no sign of any other structural failure until the bow actually began to submerge, and so with the aid of the drogue parachute *Crusader* might well have slowed to a halt before catastrophic damage could occur. Close examination of the cine films shows a spurt of water emerging from the cockpit aperture immediately before the boat disappeared in a cloud of spray, which seems fairly conclusive evidence that only at this point was the step holed; all lift from that surface was lost; and water rushed into the bow, probably destroying it by internal pressure.

The various cine films were not available until after Railton's eventual return to the USA, but Du Cane sent him copies, together with eye witness reports, and he spent a lot of time reviewing them, before coming to much the same conclusion about the sequence of events before the final nose dive. In a letter to Du Cane he commented on what he described as the extreme stability of the boat just before the crash, estimating that she was never more than about 6 inches clear of the water and was probably never subjected to more than 10g of acceleration. But he concluded that the local loading on the planing surface was far higher than they had anticipated, and this was where they had fallen down.

There was of course no record of the actual levels of acceleration, because the accelerometer lent by the Marine Aircraft Experimental Establishment was now at the bottom of Loch Ness. The loss was accepted philosophically by Smith of M.A.E.E as "another of those risks one has to take in experimental work."

A point which remained a bone of contention between Du Cane and Bray for years after was the actual existence of the waves which initiated all the trouble. These must have been caused by the wake of the *Maureen* or one of the launches, returning to their posts before the run. Such wakes may have been reflected from the steep rocky sides of the loch and back into the path of *Crusader*. The day after the accident when *Maureen* returned to the southern end of the loch, Basil Cronk pointed out to Du Cane that the wash, reflected from the shore, was still evident in the middle of the loch some 25 minutes later. However, Gordon Menzies, the son of Alec, who has spent years driving his boat on the Loch and studying wake patterns, believes that reflection was not a factor. In recent years a close study of all the available cine films indicates that there were several wave patterns involved and that *Crusader* struck more than one of these.

In his official report to the Marine Motoring Association, Bray emphasised that conditions for the run were perfect and did not admit the presence of any such waves, although Du Cane himself saw them clearly and several independent eye witnesses, including the Captain of the *Maureen*, confirmed their presence in letters which are still in his file. They are readily visible in one of the cine films, taken from high above the loch near where Du Cane was standing, but much less so in the film taken from the other side of the loch and much nearer the water level, although their effect is obvious when *Crusader* strikes them. It is therefore possible that from the deck of the *Maureen*, Bray did not see the waves before the impact. Despite the clear evidence of their presence later, he continued vehemently to deny that they existed at all, and stated that Cobb appeared to be in full control of the boat throughout the run. It is also possible that had Cobb taken the same course as previously and passed further from the shore, and the timekeepers, *Crusader* might have missed the waves altogether. However, probably nobody could have anticipated this although there seems to have been a general lack of overall command structure, and George Eyston commented that they had not held their usual briefing before the run.

Because the waves were the fundamental cause of the disaster, Du Cane naturally felt strongly about Bray's denial, and as a result, the two did not speak to each other for three years. When finally Du Cane tackled him on the subject, Bray said that he had to deny their presence at the time because he was afraid of being held responsible. Du Cane retorted that the ultimate responsibility could surely only rest with the principal participant himself. Moreover, he did not believe that the presence of the waves should be blamed on any individual; they were the result of an unfortunate chance. (None of the team had apparently realised that wakes might reflect from that shore readily, or persist for so long, although the phenomenon had been mentioned in the Inverness Courier earlier in the trial period.) He also commented that the wave which initially caused the problem was probably large enough to damage any boat travelling at that speed. The fact that *Crusader* subsequently withstood further severe buffeting before finally disintegrating indicates that despite all the guesswork and improvised reinforcement they had very nearly got the strength right. But, alas, not quite.

Nevertheless, Du Cane believed that it was better to let the whole matter rest, at least as far as the press was concerned. Ironically, there is in the file, in his handwriting and on Glen Moriston Hotel notepaper, a draft press release which he had given to Angus Barr in anticipation of the record being broken. Barr tactfully returned it to him unissued.

In the absence of any announcement the press reported that "*Scientists were baffled*", and in those days when aircraft had only recently penetrated the sound barrier there were suggestions of a mysterious (and entirely imaginary) water barrier. An even less likely theory held that an underwater spring had drawn *Crusader* down, but the prize must surely go to the astrologer who wrote to explain at length that recent eclipses, in conjunction with various signs of the zodiac at certain angles, were responsible not only for the disaster to *Crusader*, but also for the recent loss of a submarine, and for John Derry's fatal crash at Farnborough. The writer commented that the R101 airship accident had been predicted by one of his colleagues in 1930, and that *"since then there have been so many disasters that one is compelled to think that the responsible authorities did not heed the lesson to be learned from astrology."* It would seem that even today, they still have not!

The Yachting Magazines which had published Du Cane's original article on the design and construction of *Crusader* offered him a fee, which he at first decided to refuse, but then accepted and passed on to the members of the Vosper design staff who he considered had done most of the work. Whilst still reluctant to publicise further comment on the accident, he permitted himself some remarks in letters to various friends and technical associates:

"Whereas the American boat Slo-Mo-Shun was nine months before going for the record, I was pushed against my better (written) judgement to let her have a go this year, although had asked for a month's respite in which to put a few things right.

"There was not a great deal wrong with her,..... but in general terms I fear the real trouble was that the development was forced on a bit too fast, which is so often apt to happen with these privately financed ventures unfortunately.

"If poor old John had had the larger rudder fitted on the day on which he first attacked the record..., which was recommended to him by me following my first trial run in the boat, he would undoubtedly have taken the record that day.

"Please do not think for one minute that because the poor old "Crusader" came to grief I have any doubts as to its suitability as a design or as a boat. Time will show that it is an achievement to be proud of, and given a little patience, time and money, could undoubtedly have defeated the existing world record by something like 60m.p.h.

Mansour, of Jetex motor fame, wrote saying that the model of *Crusader* which he had intended to put on the market would not proceed, as he thought that in view of the accident, it would be in rather bad taste.

Du Cane would never have raised the matter in public again but for a BBC Hall of Fame television programme, transmitted in March 1958. This too failed to mention the waves which had caused all the trouble, and prompted Douglas Phillips-Birt, a distinguished Naval Architect, Marine author and yacht designer, to publish, with Du Cane's support, an article in *Shipbuilding and Shipping Record* magazine which set the record straight. For many years afterwards, Du Cane would refer anyone who enquired about *Crusader* to this article.

Just before Christmas 1952, Railton wrote to Du Cane that he expected they had both come to many conclusions as to what to do the next time – if there was one. He would, he said, be very interested and sympathetic if one of Vosper's clients commissioned another boat, and hoped that Du Cane would feel the same if one of his own wealthy clients did so. But although he discussed the possibility with one potential client and made some very tentative plans, neither he nor Du Cane ever embarked on such a project again. The field was left clear for Donald Campbell to raise the record for Britain to almost 300m.p.h. over the years between 1955 and 1967; an impressive achievement, on a limited budget, but one which Cobb and *Crusader* might well have surpassed over a decade before, if only everyone had exercised a little less haste, and a little more patience. Time has indeed shown that it was a technical achievement of which to be proud, but...

For want of a nail; shoe, horse and rider were lost...

Leddy/Castrol

*   *   *

JOHN COBB

Press Release No. 1   1st July, 1952

"CRUSADER"

My Railton-Vosper boat

This boat has been built with the object of conducting research into high-speed travel on water. Its rather revolutionary layout was originally suggested to me by Reid Railton. Design and construction have been carried out by Vosper Ltd. in co-operation with the British Aluminium Company and the de Havilland Engine Company.

We decided that the boat should be powered by a jet engine since this form of propulsion has great advantages over the conventional propeller when aiming at very high speeds. As boat-speed increases, so the efficiency of a propeller decreases until, at the highest speed so far attained on water, only about one-third of the horsepower developed by the engine can be converted into propulsive force.

With a jet engine, on the other hand, the thrust remains nearly constant, irrespective of the speed of the boat, while the overall efficiency of propulsion actually increases rapidly with the boat-speed. Moreover, at speeds approaching 200 m.p.h., the horsepower available from a jet engine of given weight and bulk is rather greater than that provided by a piston engine of the same size, even if all the latter's power could be used propulsively instead of the one-third which is actually available. The designers of the boat and I were satisfied that, provided we could master the technique of applying it to boat propulsion, a jet engine was the logical choice.

With the agreement of the Ministry of Supply, the de Havilland Engine Company has made available a Ghost engine, similar to those fitted in the D.H. Comet. The land based and carrier borne Venom fighters, which have such a big responsibility in the defence of this country over the next few years, are also fitted with this type of engine. A de Havilland Vampire, with a similar Ghost engine, still holds the World's height record of over 59,000 feet.

The novel shape of the hull was dictated by the desire to prevent its being disturbed by the very large forces which are

PRESS OFFICER: ANGUS BARR 46 GROSVENOR STREET, LONDON, W.I.

TELEPHONES	ANGUS BARR	DAY: MAYFAIR 9232	NIGHT: LEE GREEN 0130
	LAURENCE SULTAN	DAY: MAYFAIR 9232	NIGHT: BRIXTON 1678

JOHN COBB

Press Release No. 1.   Sheet No. 2.

exerted by the surrounding air on the hull of a boat travelling
at very high speed. With boats of conventional design, presenting
large, fairly flat surfaces to the air, these forces may tend to
lift (or depress) the hull to such an extent as to spoil its performance completely. Since the purpose of our project was to
achieve speeds greater than have ever been reached before, it was
obviously vital for us to avoid these forces as far as possible.

Having arrived at a shape for the hull that was satisfactory
in this respect, it was, at least, equally important to provide it
with planing-surfaces that would ensure stable running at high
speed. Lastly it was necessary to endow it with enough buoyancy
to enable it to float satisfactorily when at rest. The main
problem facing the designers has been to work out a compromise
which should satisfy these three requirements.

The design was constantly checked at successive stages by
the use of rocket-propelled models, at first by small models of
one-sixteenth scale, and finally by a large model of one-sixth
scale. This large model, propelled by a rocket of known thrust,
was actually timed to achieve a speed of 97 m.p.h. We believe
that the boat, as it now stands, represents a fundamentally sound
solution of the problem, although considerable experimentation and
development will probably be required before the final high-speed
trials are made.

The construction of such a boat is, in itself, a considerable
problem since it is necessary to obtain maximum strength with minimum weight penalty. In this case, a planned mixture of birch ply
and high strength aluminium alloy has been used. The hull and
sponsons are basically of plywood reinforced as necessary with
aluminium alloy, while the outrigger beams are almost entirely of
aluminium alloy. The actual planing surfaces are of aluminium
sheet.

The overall length of the boat is 31 feet, with a span over
the sponsons of 13 feet. The weight in running trim is expected
to be nearly three tons.

Provision has been made for the experimental use of
parachute-drogues to act as an "air-brake", in case such a thing
should be found necessary.

....

PRESS OFFICER: ANGUS BARR 46 GROSVENOR STREET, LONDON, W.I.

| TELEPHONES | ANGUS BARR | DAY: MAYFAIR 9232 | NIGHT: LEE GREEN 0130 |
| | LAURENCE SULTAN | DAY: MAYFAIR 9232 | NIGHT: BRIXTON 1678 |

JOHN COBB

Press Release No. 1.   Sheet No. 3

I should like to make special acknowledgement to
Commander Peter Du Cane of Vosper Ltd., to Reid Railton and
to the staffs of the Admiralty Experimental Station, Haslar,
the De Havilland Engine Company, C.C. Wakefield & Company Ltd.
and the Aerodynamic Section of the Fairey Aviation Company.
Finally, I acknowledge gratefully the co-operation of the
Rocket Propulsion Department of the Royal Aircraft Establishment, Farnborough which made possible the checking of our
design by high-speed model.

E N D

PRESS OFFICER: ANGUS BARR 46 GROSVENOR STREET, LONDON, W.I.

| TELEPHONES | ANGUS BARR | DAY: MAYFAIR 9232 | NIGHT: LEE GREEN 0130 |
| | LAURENCE SULTAN | DAY: MAYFAIR 9232 | NIGHT: BRIXTON 1678 |

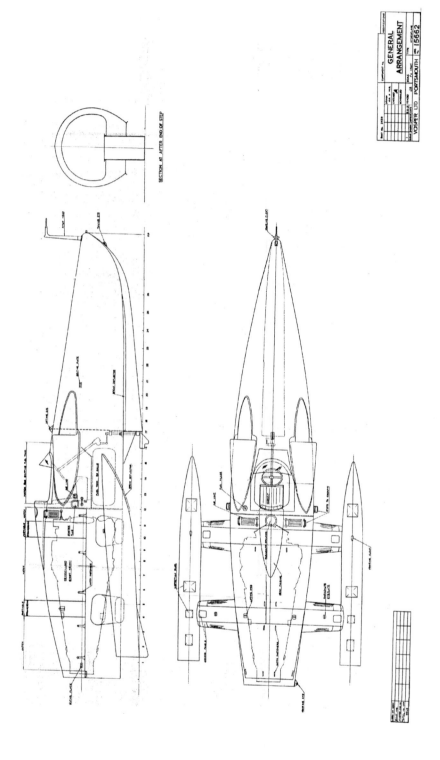

Index of People and Organisations

List of illustrations.

*   *   *